Is Capitalism Working?

The Big Idea

Jacob Field

Is Capitalism Working?

A primer for the 21st century

Over 150 illustrations

Thames & Hudson

General Editor:
Matthew Taylor

Contents

Introduction

A

Capitalism is an economic system in which the ultimate goal is profit. Goods and services are produced with the aim of making money. Defining capitalism is straightforward, but a more complex question remains: Is it working?

Answering this question requires asking many others: What has capitalism achieved for humanity? Who benefits from the system, and what is the impact if its profits are not shared out equitably? Has capitalism done anything to address social and global inequalities, or has it merely broadened them? Are there any alternatives to capitalism, and what is their efficacy? What have been the environmental consequences of capitalism, and can the system be adapted to deliver a more sustainable future?

Addressing these issues is vital because capitalism is ubiquitous, and has been since it began to emerge in its modern form more than 200 years ago (coinciding with the Industrial Revolution and the beginning of globalization) and spread across the world to become the dominant economic system. The contemporary world is inextricably linked to capitalism; it is an inescapable force that impacts everyone on the planet and reaches into every aspect of our daily lives. The first chapter of this book details how this happened by charting the evolution of modern capitalism from its roots in late 18th-century Britain all the way to the global financial crisis of 2008. It also explores how the way people thought about economics transformed during this period.

There are competing arguments regarding the success or failure of capitalism.

Ignoring one side or the other leads to a blinkered perspective that negates any possibility of a deeper understanding of how our economy operates. The second and third chapters of this book examine the two sides of the debate. Chapter 2 sets out the remarkable gains capitalism has made – leading to greater prosperity and increased standards of living and providing a framework for some of the most important innovations in history. In comparison, Chapter 3 examines the most problematic features of capitalism – how it has evolved to enrich only a closed elite, and to create unprecedented levels of inequality and possibly irretrievable damage to the environment. Adaptations, modifications and alternatives to capitalism do exist. Chapter 4 suggests some of the possible solutions that can remedy its most problematic and damaging features.

A   One of George Orwell's greatest works, *Animal Farm* (1945) is an allegory for the Russian Revolution of 1917 and the rise of Stalinism. Despite the pigs' original promise of equality, they form a dictatorship that is even more oppressive than that of their former human owners.

Industrial Revolution occurs when an economy changes from being mostly agricultural to focus more on manufacturing. It witnesses rapid economic growth and increased productivity.

Globalization is a term used to describe the process of the integration of the world that began to gather pace in the later 19th century. It encompasses economics, culture and politics.

Before delving further, some basic principles about how capitalism operates need to be set out. Firstly, within the capitalist system are economic actors. They may be individuals, companies, institutions or governments. Economic actors are broadly divided into owners and labourers. Owners possess the means of production, which may be natural resources (e. g. land) or capital goods (e.g. tangible assets). All economic actors respond to incentives, chiefly remunerative ones.

Before the 19th century, the majority of owners were individuals; now the most powerful are companies. In a capitalist system, owners tend to be private rather than government bodies. The government-run public sector is focused on services that are supposed to benefit all of society, such as infrastructure, education and health care. The private sector is ultimately based on making money for its owners. Such profit-seeking enterprises are far more diverse in the range of goods and services they provide, which means that in capitalist systems they usually employ more of the workforce and make up more of the economy.

Economic actors produce commodities that are traded through the market, which assigns them a value so exchanges can be made. The earliest markets were barter-based, before money became

A

Demand refers to how much of a commodity economic actors want to buy; supply is how much sellers can provide to the market. Theoretically, prices will vary until they reach a state of equilibrium in which the quantity demanded matches that supplied.

A   The bitcoin was launched as a worldwide digital currency in 2009. Its value against the US dollar has risen by a factor of more than 4,000 since its inception.

B   This map of the Maluku Islands (Spice Islands) is from *Theatrum Orbis Terrarum, sive, Atlas Novus* (1635) by Willem and Joan Blaeu. Although the islands are located in modern-day Indonesia, spices produced there attracted numerous European traders and colonists, particularly the Portuguese and the Dutch.

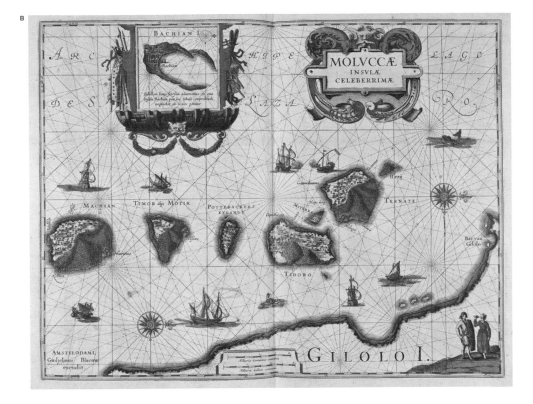

the primary means of exchange. Money began as physical cash, but this is now being replaced by digital currencies such as bitcoins.

Driving the market are supply and demand. The relationship between these two factors helps to determine prices and economic activity.

Ensuring that markets operate effectively has been a central issue for economists for centuries. When the discipline of economics first emerged in the late 18th and early 19th centuries, it was argued that governments should leave the market alone. Competition between sellers would ensure progress, because the drive to win customers would lead to the most efficient outcomes. In turn, this would increase productivity and decrease prices. It was believed that if the market were allowed to regulate itself, it would create a mutually beneficial system for owners and consumers and lead to economic growth. Chapter 1 challenges many of these assumptions.

A In use since the 1950s, container ships carry goods loaded into metal boxes. The transportation of goods in this way has dramatically cut the cost of shipping and has become one of the driving forces of globalization.
B Amazon's fulfilment centre at Rugely, England, is essentially a massive warehouse where goods are stored. It is staffed by 'pickers', who take goods from the shelves to pack and ship to customers. Online retailers use fulfilment centres to manage the dispatch and shipping of their products, leaving them free to concentrate on other areas of business.

A

A key feature of capitalism is international trade. This occurs when one country demands something from another country, because it is better quality, cheaper or locally unavailable.

Clearly, capitalism requires finance. Financial markets, operated by intermediaries such as banks, link those who require capital (borrowers) with those who have it (lenders). Without these systems, modern capitalism would be impossible. They enable capital to be invested efficiently into growing sectors, but there is a danger that this will lead to speculative behaviour by lenders seeking the best returns. Even more potentially damaging is the uncertainty that occurs when lenders lose confidence in certain sectors or countries and no longer extend credit to them.

The state has a major role to play in the success or failure of capitalism. The most important functions that it performs for capitalism are: keeping order, providing an institutional framework (e.g. through a legal system), supplying public goods (e.g. infrastructure) and assisting when markets fail. In order to pay for this, the state uses loans and taxation.

B

The basic framework of capitalism has been described, but how can it be known if it is 'working'?

Sectoral structure is one measure of development. There are three sectors: primary (using natural resources, mostly agriculture), secondary (manufacturing) and tertiary (services). In less developed economies (and most of the world before the Industrial Revolution), the majority of the population is involved in the primary sector.

By the early 20th century, there had been a global shift towards manufacturing. Since 1950, global economic activity has focused more on services such as transport and finance. As incomes rise, people tend to spend more on services and less on manufactures and food. Broadly, the wealthier and more developed the country, the higher the proportion of its population involved in the tertiary sector.

If the goal of capitalism is profit, then the simplest way to assess its success is to determine whether wealth has increased.

The measure that most economists use to gauge development is gross domestic product (GDP). This is the value of all the goods and services produced in a country, usually per year or quarter. Dividing this figure by population gives GDP per capita, which provides a better idea of how productive an economy has been. Adding together the GDPs for all countries produces gross world product, which was $75.6 trillion in 2016.

A

The **Gini coefficient** is an index that measures how income is distributed within a population, with 'zero' meaning everyone has the same income and 'one' meaning that a single person has all of the income. It was developed by the Italian statistician Corrado Gini (1884–1965).

B

A   In the early 1980s, the Sheraton hotel in the West Bay area of Doha, Qatar, was the only feature of the skyline, and the neighbouring landscape was mostly vacant and undeveloped.
B   Today, Doha is a sea of skyscrapers.
C   In the village of Gam, Central African Republic, gold-mining is the main business activity and child labour is still commonplace.
D   By contrast, most people in Norway enjoy a high standard of living and enjoy long and healthy lives.

C   D

According to the World Bank, since 1960 average world GDP per capita has grown from around $450 to over $10,000. Per capita figures are averages, and therefore mask variations of individual wealth. The Gini coefficient expresses how wealth is distributed within a nation.

Dollar figures tell only half the story.

Measures such as the human development index (HDI) reveal more about quality of life. HDI is a composite of life expectancy, education and income. According to the United Nations, Norway had the highest HDI in 2015 (0.949) and Central African Republic had the lowest (0.352). In wealthier countries, people tend to be healthier, receive better education, have a democratic voice and enjoy more personal freedom.

The ultimate measure of whether capitalism is working is to establish whether it is offering a better quality of life to the greatest number of people – not merely delivering profits to some.

This book explores how the capitalist system has both benefited and failed humanity, as well as the possible alternatives and changes that could be made to improve it.

1. How Capitalism Evolved

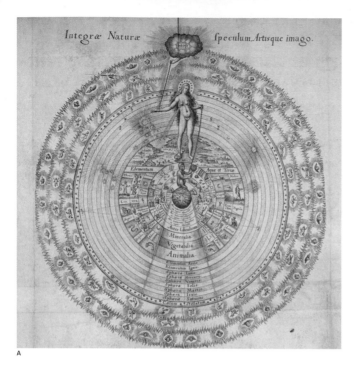

Integræ Naturæ   Speculum.Artisque imago.

A

Feudalism was a system common in medieval Europe. It created a tiered society in which everyone theoretically had a level of obligation to their superior. The majority of people, mostly peasants, owed some proportion of their labour or economic output to their local lord, who had a high degree of control over their lives.

Output is the quantity of services or goods produced by a person, thing or region.

For much of human history, economies have been virtually stagnant. The roots of global exchange had emerged by the 2nd century BC in the Silk Road, an extensive network of land and sea routes that linked Asia to Europe and remained important until the 15th century. However, most activity was agricultural, geared to subsistence or fulfilling feudal obligations.

The roots of modern capitalism emerged in Western Europe after 1500, particularly in the Dutch Republic and England. The accumulation of capital and the making of profit grew increasingly important, eventually becoming the main focus of the economy. Accompanying these changes was the growth of international trade, financial institutions, new economic theories and technologies that increased productivity. However, for the next three centuries, economic growth remained slow. Most economies grew at around 2% per decade, if that.

In many respects, a country's economy develops as a result of changes in three factors: national population, technological knowledge and institutions. During the early modern period, all three were transformed in Britain. As a result, the first Industrial Revolution (which began in the mid-18th century and ran until the *c.* 1830s) occurred there.

This process can be seen as a shift from an organic economy to an inorganic one. Organic economies are largely based on human and animal muscle, and machines that can be powered by them. These were supplemented by devices that harnessed natural sources of energy such as wind and water (e.g. windmills and waterwheels). The fixed quantity of land and the resources that can be extracted from it limit growth. Theoretically, inorganic economies are capable of much faster growth because they are reliant on mechanical energy from mined mineral sources, such as coal and petroleum. Machines, if well-maintained, have a theoretically constant output.

A   *The Great Chain of Being*
(1617) by Robert Fludd
illustrates the idea that
everything in the universe
– humans, animals, plants
and minerals – can be
classified and placed
in a hierarchical order.

B   This illustration from the
August calendar page of
The Queen Mary Psalter
(*c.* 1310) shows a reeve
directing his serfs to
harvest the corn. Profits
from agriculture remained
low or non-existent, as
well as subject to the
vagaries of the weather,
for the next five centuries.

From the early 17th to the late 18th centuries, the Enlightenment and Scientific Revolution took place in the West. This contributed to a major shift in intellectual and philosophical life, and the fostering of a more rational world view. Systemization made it easier to disseminate knowledge, thus enabling the spread of new ideas, and also their refinement and adaptation.

B

The most important developments were the invention of the steam engine and the mechanization of textile production, both of which occurred first in Britain. These fields were pursued only because they were potentially profitable. This is because wages in Britain in the 17th century were comparatively higher than in other areas, so labour was expensive for business owners. There was an incentive to invent and to use labour-saving devices that did not exist in areas where labour was cheaper, such as in India or China.

The first steam engines were designed in the late 17th and early 18th centuries to pump water, but their motions were too imprecise to drive machinery. They were also expensive to operate because they were fuel inefficient. It was not until the 1760s and 1770s that a steam engine with a rotary motion smooth enough to run machinery was developed. Over the next century, this design was improved and adapted constantly. In 1760 only 6% of the 85,000 horsepower produced by stationary power sources in Britain came from steam. However, by 1907 stationary power sources in the country were producing 9,842,000 horsepower, and 98% came from steam.

A Interior, Woman by a Spinning Wheel (1868) by Knud Larsen Bergslien. Before mechanization, spinning fibres such as wool to make yarn was one of the main female occupations, and most women worked in their own homes.

B An Iron Forge (1772) by Joseph Wright of Derby. During the 18th century, new techniques to produce iron were invented in England, which led to better quality iron at a lower cost.

C During the 19th and early 20th centuries, Wales was one of the leading coal-producing areas in the world. This image depicts the pit head, winding gear and coal trucks at a colliery at Ponsy Pool in Monmouth, Wales, in 1888.

D Some coal mines allowed unemployed people to look through their waste tips to gather free coal. This photograph was taken in 1936 at Cilfynydd near Pontypridd in the South Wales valleys.

A

B

C

D

Cheap coal was crucial because it meant that steam power's initial inefficiency was less costly. Britain was the first country to harness coal's power for industry, having abundant natural deposits to draw on, and by 1800 it produced 90% of the world's coal.

Starting with the textile industry, the Industrial Revolution transformed manufacturing. From the mid-18th century, a series of inventions led to the full steam-driven mechanization of textile production in Britain only a century later, and productivity skyrocketed.

A

In 1750 approximately 100,000 operative hours were required to process 100 pounds of cotton. By the early 19th century, it took only 100 hours. The techniques used in textile production were replicated in other industries, such as metals and pottery, and in other countries (Belgium was the first in mainland Europe to adapt the technology). What started out as an endeavour to produce textiles more cheaply eventually transformed society. Mechanical devices were too large and expensive for domestic use. Consequently, it was more cost-effective to centralize manufacturing into factories, where economies of scale decreased costs. This contributed to urbanization as factories tended to be located in towns, which were close to labour supplies, markets and transport hubs.

Previously, workers operated at their own pace and set their own hours, but in factories, employers regulated hours and conditions. Division of labour meant workers became more specialized in order to maximize their output. During this time, growing agricultural productivity – driven by new techniques and more efficient land use – freed up labour to work in manufacturing.

A   *Spinners in a Cotton Mill* (1911) by Lewis Hine depicts child workers at a textile mill. Hine's photographs were a major factor in forcing the US government to pass laws regulating child labour.
B   From 1763 to 1775, James Watt and his business partner Matthew Boulton developed a steam engine that was far more efficient than previous designs, and also provided a smooth rotary motion.

Improvements in transport were vital to this burgeoning industrialization, allowing both raw materials and manufactured goods to be distributed more cheaply and quickly. After the 1830s, a new mode of transport took off in Britain: the steam-powered railway. This made transport more reliable and decreased travel times, thereby increasing capacity. Other nations also developed their own railway lines. They were used most dramatically in the USA, which in 1830 had 75 miles (120 km) of track. By 1890 it had 164,000 miles (263,933 km). Improvements in transport lowered the costs of raw materials for producers and of finished goods for consumers.

Businesses could sell in markets where previously transport costs would have made their products too expensive compared to ones made locally. This encouraged regional specialization and competition.

B

STEAM ENGINE.

Boulton and Watt's Engine on the original Construction.

Economies of scale occur when enterprises increase in size or efficiency. As outputs increase, prices per unit decline because fixed costs are spread out. Economies of scale are vital to long-term success. They are more durable than a technological edge, which can disappear with new innovations, or consumer loyalty (new customers are always available).

Division of labour is the breakdown of an economic system into different tasks, each of which is carried out by a worker who concentrates on their specific assignment.

The final major ingredients of the Industrial Revolution were institutions, the structures that humans impose on the world to produce their desired outcomes. They encompass a variety of arrangements between economic actors, including political systems, legal codes and financial bodies.

Britain developed flexible institutions that encouraged the increase of productivity rather than merely the redistribution of income. This led to a decline in rent-seeking activities. The first major set of institutions was the state and legal system. By the late 17th century, England's Parliament had the greatest powers of any representative body in Europe, which meant that the country was not governed by the whims of an absolute monarch. English common law placed a strong emphasis on property rights, including the rights to reap the benefits of intellectual innovation.

A

B

C

Rent-seeking refers to economic actions and policies that aim to increase the wealth of an economic actor without increasing overall wealth. For example, when an industry or company lobbies a government to pass laws and regulations that limit competition this could be described as rent-seeking, because the industry or company is aiming to maintain its profits and market share without having to offer an improved service or lower prices.

Common law is the basis of the British legal system, and also of those in the Commonwealth and the USA. Many historians believe common law is ideal for creating favourable conditions for economic growth because it emphasizes individual property rights and is based on decisions made by relatively independent judiciary, which add flexibility.

D

The second major set of institutions was financial. In 1694 the Bank of England was incorporated as the banker for the British government by issuing bonds. The following year it began the permanent issue of banknotes, which promised to pay the bearer on demand the value of the note in bullion.

A   Share certificate (1606) for the Dutch
    East India Company (VOC), one of the
    oldest such documents in the world.
B   Banknote (1699) for £555, issued by
    the Bank of England.
C   Before reforms in 1844, private banks in
    Britain could issue their own notes, such
    as this one for the Berwick Bank from 1818.
D   The Amsterdam Stock Exchange (1611)
    was constructed to house traders dealing
    in stocks and bonds, first for the VOC
    and then for other companies. It remained
    in use until it was demolished in 1835.

Bonds are a way in which companies or governments are loaned money. The holder of the bond is the lender, and the issuer is the borrower. The 'coupon' is the interest that the borrower has to pay to the lender, as well as the date when the loan has to be repaid.

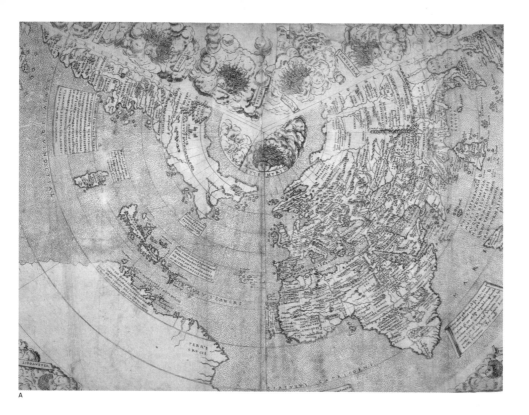

A

Banknotes made transactions more straightforward, although they were only trusted if people thought the bank that issued them had sufficient bullion to back the amounts in circulation.

When consumer confidence failed, so did the bank.

Shares and the means to trade them were also vital. They diversified risk and broadened the base of investment. In joint stock companies, which were founded in England in the mid-16th century, shares (also referred to as equities) could be bought by investors. They then owned a part of the company in proportion to the shares they had purchased. England's first stock exchange was among London's coffee houses, and a formal stock exchange in Amsterdam opened in 1611 (the London Stock Exchange was officially formed in 1801).

As capitalism gathered pace, the European 'Age of Discovery' began. From the 1490s, and over the next four centuries, European powers established colonial regimes in the Americas, Africa, Oceania and Asia. The prime motives were economic: overseas colonies provided raw materials, such as cotton, sugar and tea, that were unavailable in Europe, as well as a guaranteed market for their manufactured goods. The first wave of European imperialism occurred in the Americas. Spanish and Portuguese colonial regimes there were extractive and focused primarily on the mining of precious metals.

Contact with Europeans was highly damaging to indigenous societies, particularly in the Americas. Diseases such as smallpox and influenza swept through these populations because they had no natural immunity. Death rates of more than 90% occurred in some areas.

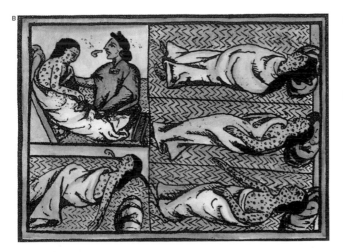

A   This Planisphere (1506), designed by Giovanni Matteo Contarini and engraved by Francesco Rosselli, was the first printed map of the world to illustrate parts of the American continent.

B   Bernardino de Sahagún's 16th-century *Florentine Codex* manuscript records his investigation of Meso-American society. It includes more than 2,000 illustrations by indigenous artists, such as the depiction of the outbreak of small pox, a disease brought over by the Spanish.

By the mid-18th century, Spain and Portugal ruled most of Latin America while Britain, France and Spain vied for dominance in North America. By 1800 Western powers controlled 35% of the world's land surface; by 1914 this had risen to 85%, mostly due to imperial expansion in Africa and Asia.

The Atlantic slave trade grew alongside European imperialism.

In 1502 the first African slaves were sent to the New World, where they mostly laboured in mines and plantations. Before 1600, some 2,000 slaves left Africa per year, increasing to *c.* 20,000 by the 17th century and peaking at *c.* 88,000 by the 1780s. The 'Atlantic System' took shape, and European ships made three-legged

A

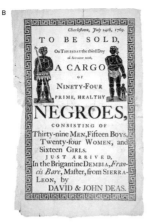

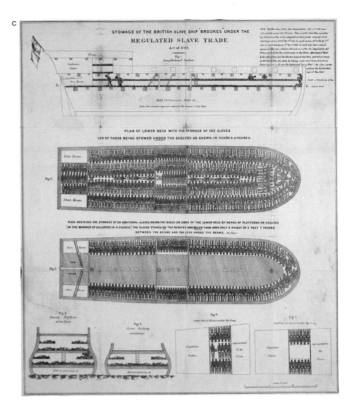

A   One of James Gillray's best-known political satires, *The Plumb-Pudding in Danger* (c. 1818) depicts French Emperor Napoléon Bonaparte and British Prime Minister William Pitt the Younger greedily carving up the world.
B   A handbill for an auction of 'prime healthy' slaves in South Carolina in 1769.
C   Published by abolitionists in 1788, this image of the British slave ship *Brookes* illustrates how 400 slaves were packed into the ship. It was widely reproduced to show the horrific conditions of the transatlantic slave trade.

voyages: they carried manufactured goods from Europe to Africa, took slaves from Africa to the Americas (where they sold at a double or triple profit) and transported raw materials (especially tobacco, sugar and cotton) produced by slave labour back to Europe. European colonies in North America traded directly with Africa and the Caribbean.

By the time slavery had been abolished in North America, 12 million Africans had been enslaved and sent across the Atlantic. Some 4 million died before they arrived as the conditions on the Middle Passage were brutal and inhumane. Mortality aboard ship sometimes reached 50%.

European powers became more involved in Asia, eager to access its textiles and spices. Joint stock companies were set up to trade there, notably the English and Dutch East India Companies (established in 1600 and 1602, respectively). The English East India Company rose to become a colonial power in its own right, directly ruling most of the Indian subcontinent until 1858. Although China and Japan were not formally colonized, from 1839 European powers used military threat to force them to sign a series of 'unequal treaties', which unilaterally opened them up to trade. Imperialism was a necessary, but not sufficient, condition for industrialization. Spain and Portugal's economies both stagnated, whereas Britain took full economic advantage of overseas trade.

The way that people thought about the economy was changing.

Before the late 18th century, governments viewed the economy in terms of mercantilism. They measured wealth by reserves of bullion, which was achieved through a positive balance of trade. Economic policies subsidized local production and set tariffs (taxes on imports or exports) on foreign goods.

A

A   *Lord Clive Meeting with Mir Jafar After the Battle of Plassey* (c. 1762) by Francis Hayman depicts the aftermath of the pivotal battle in 1757, when the East India Company's victory laid the foundations of British imperial dominance over the Indian subcontinent.
B   On the obverse of this Scottish trade token from Kirkcaldy (1797) is Adam Smith, who was born there in 1723.
C   The reverse shows an industrial scene with the title of his master work, *The Wealth of Nations.*

Such views fell away towards the end of the 18th century. The work of Scottish economist Adam Smith formed the basis of the classical school of economics, which argued that if individuals were left to their own devices, everyone would benefit.

Smith used the metaphor the 'invisible hand'. Although he used this phrase only three times in his writings, it has nonetheless become a highly influential concept. It refers to the argument that people's individual actions, even if pursued in the spirit of self-interest, can benefit wider society. This has become a vital justification for arguing that the unfettered development of capitalism will ultimately be positive for society.

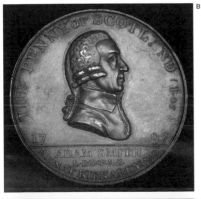

B

C

Mercantilism was the dominant economic theory in the West between the 15th and the mid-18th centuries. It stressed that nations should enrich themselves at the expense of their neighbours. A major feature of this type of economy was rent-seeking.

Balance of trade is the difference between the value of the goods and services that a nation exports and imports. If a country has a trade deficit, it imports a greater value of goods than it exports. The opposite is a trade surplus. Balance of payments is a broader term that includes all financial transactions between a country and the rest of the world.

Adam Smith (1723–90) was a philosopher and political economist (the latter term describes the discipline of economics as it was known at that time). In 1776 he published *The Wealth of Nations*, the first modern work of economics.

A key theory in the classical school was the 'law of markets', put forward by French economist Jean-Baptiste Say (1767–1832). This states that 'a product is no sooner created than it…affords a market for other products to the full extent of its own value'. Production will create wages and income, which will increase wealth and lead to demand. Classical economists argued that the government should be as non-interventionist as possible. This laissez-faire approach suggested that a free market (where the forces of supply and demand ultimately determine prices and the government does not intervene too much) would produce the most efficient returns.

An important influence was utilitarianism, which argued that the utility of an action should be judged by its results, most importantly an overall increase in well-being. Applied to economics, this meant that an action could be regarded as positive even if it negatively impacted on some of the population.

The neoclassical school of economics, which developed in the 1890s, shared the classical school's belief that markets should generally be left alone. Both schools theorized that economic actors are rational, motivated by self-interest to maximize wealth and to meet their goals in the most efficient way possible (the behaviouralist school later challenged this assumption). Classical and neoclassical economics differed in other ways, though. First, classical economists measured the value of a product according to how much labour time went into producing it; this is known as the 'labour theory of value'.

A   Passengers crowd onto a train in Loni, a town in Uttar Pradesh in northern India. Since India won independence in 1947, the Indian population has nearly quadrupled. This rapid growth rate has only been possible since India industrialized, because rising real wages, prosperity and development have led to a decrease in mortality, particularly for infants.

B   This illustration for H. G. Wells's *The War of the Worlds* was produced in 1906 by Henrique Alvim Corrêa. The novel, published in 1898, drew on the popular fears about the uncertainties of a fully industrialized world.

The **behaviouralist school** does not assume that economic actors are rational, but focuses on modelling how humans actually behave. It argues that humans are emotional beings who rely on heuristics (practical methods to simplify decision-making) and framing (pre-existing biases), which affect economic behaviour.

Externalities are outcomes that are not borne by the economic actor responsible for them. They can be negative (e.g. pollution made by factories) or positive (e.g. when a company develops a new technology that increases overall productivity). Many externalities are negative. They can be addressed by governments through regulation or by imposing taxes on economic actors equal to the value of the negative externality.

Real wages are adjusted for inflation, and so accurately represent the goods and services that they can purchase.

B

Neoclassical economists stressed the 'subjective theory of value', which stated that values are relative and based on preferences. Significantly, through the study of externalities, some neoclassical economists questioned the free market. They argued that there were some situations in which government intervention in the capitalist system was necessary (e.g. during financial crises).

After 1820 capitalism took off in Western Europe and North America. World population exploded, partly due to the Industrial Revolution; the average age of first marriage fell at this time, which meant that people had more children and the birth rate rose. The rise in real wages had enabled people to marry earlier and to set up their own households. Before the 19th century, whenever populations increased real wages decreased because more labour was available.

By the second half of the 19th century, wages were increasing at the same time as the population for the first time. The potential Malthusian crisis was arrested.

Life expectancy at birth increased rapidly. In 1800 the global average was around 30 years of age. From 2010 to 2013, average global life expectancy at birth was 71. This contributed to a huge rise in population. In 1800 the world's population was around one billion. It hit seven billion in 2011, and will reach eight billion by 2024.

Technological innovations accelerated during the 19th century. Steam power was adopted for ships, enabling faster, more reliable oceanic crossings at higher capacity than sail-powered

A   Workers make their final inspections of carbon arc lamps before packing at the Hammersmith Lamp and Valve Works, London, in 1903. The invention of electric lighting transformed the economy, allowing factories and businesses to remain open around the clock.
B   At the Ford River Rouge Complex in Dearborn, Michigan, completed in 1928, Ford cars were assembled, from the initial chassis to the finished vehicle, and driven off the line under their own power.

Malthusian crisis was named after British demographer Thomas Robert Malthus (1766–1834). He believed that unchecked population growth would lead to a decline in health and individual income, and would eventually cause a crisis. This could be prevented by reducing populations through the 'positive check' (famine, war or disease) and the 'preventative check' (contraception or delaying having children).

A

B

vessels had offered previously. The means to generate electricity and to convert it into light or mechanical energy were discovered, too. Electricity was also used to send messages via telegraph, thereby creating a global communication system. These developments in transport and communication meant globalization gathered momentum.

In 1862 the first mass-market internal combustion engine was designed, followed by the first automobile in 1886. Electrification and improved engines facilitated mass production. Factories began to use moving assembly lines, with each worker assigned a specific repetitive task. This increased efficiency. For example, by 1914 the Ford factory in Michigan, USA, could produce a Model T automobile in 93 minutes of labour time. These techniques lowered production costs and therefore prices.

A

Although the Industrial Revolution had started in Britain, by the end of the 19th century the country was no longer the 'workshop of the world'. By 1900 both Germany and the USA had greater total industrial outputs.

Capitalism's achievements were not evenly distributed. For many people, the Industrial Revolution led to longer working hours in noisy and unsafe factories, as well as relocation to cramped filthy cities. Early socialism, which developed in the 1820s and 1830s, criticized the relentless striving for profit and advocated the creation of egalitarian societies with communal ownership of resources and commodities.

Karl Marx (1818–83) and Friedrich Engels (1820–95), German socialist philosophers exiled to London because of their political beliefs, created the most significant anti-capitalist philosophy. The Marxist School viewed society as based on classes rather than individuals, and class conflict as the driving force of history. Capitalism was just one stage of human development, to be replaced by a socialist society in which the economy was planned centrally by the state. In order to achieve this, the working classes needed to overthrow the capitalist system through revolution.

World War I (1914–18) destroyed the optimistic outlook that global capitalism would create peace through commercial links between nations. Military deaths totalled 11 million and civilian deaths 7 million. But perhaps the most important long-term outcome of the conflict was the Russian Revolution of 1917, which led to the establishment of the USSR. There, the means of production were owned either by the state or by workers' cooperatives. Central planning of the economy was imposed, and rapid industrialization was forced on what had previously been an undeveloped, mainly agricultural economy. In its first decades, the Soviet economy grew spectacularly, although in the long term it revealed major weaknesses (see Chapter 2).

B

C

A

Meanwhile in the USA, the Roaring Twenties was a decade of prosperity and the stock market soared.

However, on 24 October 1929, there was a huge crash on the New York Stock Exchange as investors lost confidence in the value of shares. The economic bubble burst. Financial instability spread worldwide, hoarding of assets prevented investment and there was a global collapse in demand. These events led to the Great Depression, the greatest financial crisis of the 20th century.

A   Capturing the zeitgeist of the Roaring Twenties, large crowds leave the theatres close to Times Square, New York, in the mid-1920s.
B   Margaret Bourke-White's photograph of a queue at a relief station during the 1937 Ohio River flood, one of the worst disasters of the Great Depression era, captures the discord between reality and the idealized 'American dream'.

An **economic bubble** occurs when the price of an asset greatly exceeds its intrinsic value. It is usually the result of over-confidently and artificially inflating prices.

It caused a breakdown of international trade, a global decline of economic output (from 1929 to 1932, world GDP fell by 15%) and mass unemployment (30 million in the USA alone). Recovery did not begin until 1933. As a result of the Great Depression, many in Europe turned to political extremists promising radical solutions. In Germany this contributed to the rise of the Nazi Party, which took power in 1933. The Great Depression was followed by World War II (1939–45), which involved 92 countries and 121 million military personnel. The conflict cost around 70 million lives, more than two-thirds of them civilian.

B

A

B

Despite the devastation caused by World War II, the conflict was followed by an economic boom that lasted until 1973. During this 'golden age of capitalism', annual per capita incomes grew in the USA by 2.5%, in Western Europe by more than 4%, and in Japan by more than 8%. Governments enacted Keynesian policies, which encouraged financial stability and high employment. In many countries, important industries such as railways or energy were nationalized and generous systems of public welfare were created. The institutional foundations for the international post-war economy were laid at the Bretton Woods Conference, which took place in July 1944 in New Hampshire, USA. The meetings resulted in the establishment of the International Monetary Fund (IMF) and the World Bank.

Recovery in Western Europe was also helped by US aid from the Marshall Plan. Exchange rate stability was fixed by countries agreeing to peg the value of their currencies to the US dollar (e.g. £1 was equal to $2.80), which was trusted because of the strength of the US economy and the fact that the currency was convertible to gold. In 1947 the General Agreement on Tariffs and Trade (GATT) was signed, the first of a series of 'rounds' of agreements that reduced trade barriers between its signatories, which gradually increased in number from 23 to 123 nations by 1994.

European economies integrated with the creation of the European Coal and Steel Community between West Germany, France, Italy, the Netherlands, Belgium and Luxembourg in 1951. Six years later, they concluded a free-trade agreement – the Treaty of Rome – and created the European Economic Community (Britain joined in 1973).

Keynesian policies are named after the British economist John Maynard Keynes (1883–1946). He argued that aggregate demand was the most important economic force. The Keynesian school's most influential belief is that governments should be highly involved in macroeconomic policy (dealing with the economy as a whole) as opposed to microeconomic policy (which deals with individuals and businesses). During recessions in particular, governments should increase spending and lower taxes to maintain demand.

World Bank is an institution whose aim is to reduce poverty by providing funding and knowledge to help sustainable economic growth in developing countries. Since 1947 it has provided funding, through grants or loans with favourable terms, for more than 12,000 projects.

The **International Monetary Fund** was founded with the aim of monitoring and supervising the international economy and ensuring its stability. It has 189 members, each assigned a 'quota' based on its economic strength, which decides its maximum financial commitment, voting power and access to IMF money (in 2016 it had funds totalling $668 billion). The IMF provides bailouts to countries unable to make up their balance of payments (albeit with many conditions – particularly public spending cuts). These loans allow countries to avoid financial collapse.

The **Marshall Plan** was a programme that saw the USA provide in the region of $13 billion from 1948 to 1952 to help rebuild Western Europe. It was named after George Marshall (1880–1959), the US secretary of state at the time. The Soviet-led Eastern Bloc refused this assistance.

c

A   By 1923 the impact of hyperinflation was evident. Germany experienced rapid price inflation because the government was forced to print more paper money to buy foreign currency to pay off war reparations. Essentially, banknotes became worthless.

B   Due to the collapse of the German mark's value, it was cheaper to paper a wall with banknotes than to buy wallpaper. International organizations such as the IMF work with countries to prevent such financial disasters occurring.

C   Delegates from 44 nations attended the Bretton Woods Conference at Mount Washington Hotel in 1944.

The other feature of this period was decolonization. Most former European colonies gained independence, often after violent struggle (such as in Vietnam and Algeria). This could lead to new challenges, as in some African countries, but in general these newly independent nations enjoyed a measure of economic growth as a result of industrialization and the adoption of new technologies. Growth was particularly high in the East Asian 'tiger economies' of South Korea, Hong Kong, Singapore and Taiwan. This was because their governments enacted effective economic policies that encouraged stability, such as improving the reliability of banks. They also invested in their populations through universal primary schooling and expanding secondary and tertiary education, thereby increasing the skill of the workforce. In these countries, the state worked with private companies by sharing information and providing subsidies to certain industries (e.g. clothing, plastics, electronics and automobile manufacture). This meant that these countries' economies grew rapidly through exporting finished goods across the world.

The post-war boom stalled in the early 1970s. In 1971 the USA cancelled the convertibility of their dollar into gold, thus diminishing global trust in the currency. Countries ceased tying exchange rates to the US dollar, which led to an increased likelihood of instability as currencies now 'floated' depending on demand.

A

B

A   Early morning queues form at a gas station in Oregon in 1973 during
    the first oil crisis. Fuel was sold on a first-come, first-served basis
    and was limited to five gallons per car.
B   In some states, rationing was based on licence plate. Plates ending
    in odd numbers could buy fuel on odd-numbered days of the month,
    and those ending with even numbers on even days. However, as the
    1973 oil crisis continued, many stations were forced to close.

Crisis came in 1973, when Middle Eastern oil-producing countries launched an embargo in response to US support for Israel. It remained in place for six months, during which time the price of oil rose from $3 to $12 per barrel. A second oil crisis in 1979 occurred in the aftermath of the Iranian Revolution. These crises led to inflation and caused global recessions from 1974 to 1975 and from 1980 to 1983. This unprecedented mixture of recession and rising prices is known as 'stagflation'; traditionally, it was believed that prices would decline during recessions.

 caption text:
LA BOUR STILL ISN'T WORKING

UNEMPLOYMENT OFFICE

BRITAIN'S BETTER OFF WITH THE CONSERVATIVES.

A

From the late 1970s to the 1990s, many countries – particularly Britain and the USA – passed a series of neoliberal economic reforms. Neoliberalism aimed to reduce the government's role in the economy and to empower the private sector. Although they differed by nation, these reforms usually included privatization of state-owned enterprises, deregulation and tax cuts for the wealthy. Social welfare was reduced, as it was believed that this would encourage the poor to work harder.

These reforms were based on supply-side economic theories. They argued that the key to economic growth was to lower barriers on the production of goods and services, which would increase supply and lower costs. As a result, businesses would expand and the increased wealth of the elite would 'trickle down' to the rest of society because they would spend more. But many of these assumptions proved to be false.

The policies led to economic growth and increased prosperity for some, but this wealth was not shared evenly and in the long term contributed to financial instability (see Chapter 3).

Events in Japan illustrate how the successes of the 1980s did not last. During this decade, the Japanese economy boomed, and values of shares and property soared (at the bubble's peak, it was suggested that the 340-hectare imperial grounds in Tokyo were worth more than all of the real estate in California combined). However, the boom was not sustained in the 1990s, known as the 'lost decade' in Japan, when values collapsed alongside GDP and real wages.

The beginning of the end of the Cold War was marked by the fall of the Berlin Wall in 1989. Two years later, the USSR collapsed.

As the socialist bloc began to implode, many previously socialist economies made the transition to capitalism.

B

A Saatchi & Saatchi designed the poster for the Conservative Party's general election campaign in 1979. The Tories' victory over the Labour Party made Margaret Thatcher prime minister and she remained in power for 11 years. Her neoliberal policies fundamentally altered Great Britain.

B The fall of the Berlin Wall was announced on 9 November 1989. The Wall had symbolized the barrier between the capitalist West and communist East, and its destruction presaged the end of the Cold War and the collapse of the Eastern Bloc.

Neoliberalism built on the liberalism of the 19th century. In general, it emphasises the importance of laissez-faire economics and places a great deal of faith in free markets as the best route towards prosperity.

In many nations, this process was traumatic, with high unemployment and inflation. Russia in particular suffered; its GDP declined by 40% in seven years. China, whose communist regime was established in 1949, remained theoretically socialist, although after 1978 it gradually opened up to trade with capitalist nations.

During the 1990s, globalization and economic integration continued. In 1993 the European Union (EU) was created, establishing a common market with freedom of movement of goods, services, people and money. The EU expanded to include formerly communist countries in Eastern Europe, and comprised 28 members by 2004 (19 of which use a common currency, the euro). Membership will be reduced by one when Britain withdraws, as a result of the Brexit referendum of 2016.

In 1994 the North American Free Trade Agreement reduced trade barriers between Canada, Mexico and the USA. The following year, the World Trade Organization (WTO) replaced GATT. It has a wider scope and greater sanctioning powers than its predecessor and acts as an international forum for making trade deals and settling disputes. When Afghanistan joined the WTO in 2016, it became the 164th member, which means that the organization now represents 98% of world trade.

A

A   At the Extraordinary
     European Council meeting
     in Brussels on 29 October
     1993, delegates announced
     their approval for the
     implementation of the
     Maastricht Treaty (1992),
     which laid the foundations
     for the creation of the EU.
B   Protesters gathered at the
     WTO Ministerial Conference
     in Seattle in 1999. The
     meetings were eclipsed by
     the size, scale and violence
     of the demonstrations
     against globalization.

B

As the world economy grew more integrated, the Internet revolutionized communication, thus fostering further globalization.

By the late 1990s, national economies were bound together closely, which meant that a financial crisis could spread rapidly. The Asian financial crisis of 1997 illustrated this risk. The previously buoyant economies of South Korea, Thailand, Malaysia and Indonesia all crashed after confidence in their over-valued markets collapsed, along with their currencies. The IMF provided a bailout of $40 billion to stabilize the situation, but the crisis spread across the rest of East Asia. In turn, this contributed to the financial crises in Russia, Brazil and Argentina in 1998. In response, the anti-globalization movement gathered pace, symbolized in 1999 by the protests in Seattle, USA, against a WTO meeting there.

A

The growing ubiquity of the Internet led to the value of shares in IT companies increasing rapidly after 1995. But between 1999 and 2001, the dot-com bubble collapsed and wiped out $6 trillion of shares. Shares in theGlobe.com, a social networking service, indicate how dramatic this collapse was. When they were first offered for sale on 13 November 1998, their value increased by more than 600% in one day to $63.50. By 2001 they were worth less than one dollar and could be purchased for as little as 7 cents. The company ceased operations in 2008.

The new millennium began with recessions in most of Europe (Britain was an exception and the USA, and continued economic problems in Japan.

A   At the March for Health, Homes, Jobs and Education in London in 2016, demonstrators demanded an end to the Conservative Party's austerity policies.
B   In 2012 thousands gathered in London to protest against government cuts. Some wore the stylized Guy Fawkes mask that has become a hallmark of many protest groups.

Optimism and growth returned to most of the world during the mid 2000s, when it was believed that a new era of permanent stability had emerged. However, the global financial crisis of 2008 caused a shuddering reverse (see Chapter 3). It remains, even after a decade, the most important shaping force of the contemporary economy.

B

2. How Modern Capitalism Works

A

Capitalism works. The fact you are reading this book is proof.

Whether you purchased this book in a shop, had it delivered or are reading it electronically, it is the culmination of a series of complex interconnected processes that involved thousands of individuals. At each stage of production, economic self-interest was motivating each person.

This is not a new concept. In 1958 US businessman Leonard E. Read used the example of a pencil to show how manufacturing a simple object is the result of a vast network of people. It is not a sense of cooperation that brings them together but the quest for profit. However, in the act of enriching themselves, individuals can generate huge benefits for consumers. By striving to maximize profits and increase productivity, better goods are made more cheaply and more efficiently. This is economist Adam Smith's 'invisible hand' in action (see Chapter 1). Such a market force is unobservable yet powerful – if allowed, it guides the supply and demand of goods to the benefit of society as a whole.

By and large, romanticizing the past is a mistake. Before the 19th century and the invisible hand of capitalism, the lives of most people were tough, monotonous and short.

For centuries, the vast majority of humans eked out a precarious living in agriculture. Almost all farming was at subsistence level, so families were only a failed harvest away from starvation. Economic growth was near-undetectable. From 1000 to 1820, per capita incomes grew by just under 0.13% per year. People were not particularly healthy or long-lived either. One in three babies born died before their first birthdays, which lowered the average life expectancy to around 30 years of age.

Leonard E. Read (1898–1983) was one of the most influential proponents of libertarian thought in the 20th century. A prolific author, his best-known work is his essay 'I, Pencil' (1958).

Per capita income is the measure of the average income in a particular area (usually a nation), calculated by dividing the total income by the population. It indicates how wealthy an area is.

A   *The Gleaners* (1857) by Jean-François Millet depicts three female peasants gathering leftover stalks of wheat after the harvest. In many parts of Europe, gleaning was one of the main ways poor people could supplement their diet.
B   *Coming Home From the Marshes* (c. 1886) by Peter Henry Emerson shows agricultural workers from the Norfolk Fens in eastern England. Emerson's work provided a lasting record of rural life in the 19th century.

B

Worldwide, the average infant can now expect to live to over 70 years of age. People are living longer and richer lives than at any other point in history. Scottish-born economist Sir Angus Deaton calls this shift the 'great escape'. He argues that since 1945 'rapid economic growth in many countries has delivered hundreds of millions of people from destitution'.

This dramatic transition, unheralded in human history, is due primarily to the forces unleashed by capitalism. The number of child deaths worldwide has decreased every year for the past 50 years. In China and India, which contain more than one-third of the world's population, newborns can expect to live for 75 and 65 years, respectively. Improvements are still being felt. According to the World Health Organization, in 1990 12.6 million children under the age of five died every year. By 2015 this figure had fallen by more than half to 5.9 million.

A Combine harvesters have dramatically reduced the time and labour needed for arable farming as the header of the combine automatically cuts and gathers the crop. The larger the header, the more efficient the harvesting.
B The pressure of competition in capitalist society drives innovation. Volkswagen's glass car silos at the Autostadt in Wolfsburg, Germany, each house 800 vehicles. Cars can be delivered to purchasers automatically, by elevator, so the odometer still reads '0' at collection.

Sir Angus Deaton (b. 1945) won the Nobel Memorial Prize in Economic Sciences in 2015 and was knighted the following year. His work explores poverty, health, inequality and economic development.

A

Unsurprisingly, money leads to happiness.

According to data collected for the United Nations' 2017 World Happiness Report, there is a strong correlation between a country's GDP per capita and self-assessed life satisfaction.

Capitalism encourages innovation. The Industrial Revolution sprang to life in 18th-century Britain when textile manufacturers invested in labour-saving devices to cut costs and increase earnings. Across all sectors of the economy processes were mechanized, which reduced costs and saved time while increasing output. This continued throughout the 19th and 20th centuries.

Over the past century, farming has become increasingly efficient: between 1930 and 2000, US agricultural output quadrupled. This growth in output is due to technological innovation, which has increased the amount of food that can be produced while decreasing the labour required. As recently as 1900, it took 38 worker hours to plant, grow and harvest one acre of corn. It now takes less than three hours. Technology has thus freed billions of humans from the drudgery of manual labour. In 2000 the average GDP per capita was 30 times higher than the figure for 1800, which was about $200.

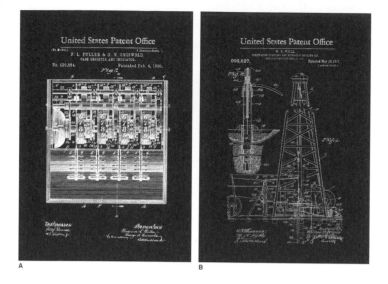

A   Investment in innovation can be highly lucrative, and inventors protect themselves by applying for patents, which give them exclusive rights over their designs. This patent (1890) is for a cash register design by Frederick L. Fuller.

B   This patent was issued by the US Patent Office in 1911. It is for a combination standard and hydraulic drilling rig by Wilson B. Wigle.

C   Incremental innovation can also be very lucrative. The first generation Apple iPhone was launched in 2007, and the billionth iPhone was sold in 2016.

A

B

The first major economist to recognize the role technological change played in economic growth was none other than Karl Marx (see Chapter 1). His prediction that capitalism was doomed to collapse, however, has proved less prescient.

In the mid-20th century, economist Joseph Schumpeter (argued that new technologies were the basis for the dynamism of capitalism. Although other factors, such as labour and finance, are also vital, it would be foolhardy to deny the importance of innovation. Schumpeter used the metaphor 'the gale of creative destruction', which he derived from Marxist economists, to describe how the economy was subject to constant waves of change due to innovations. This process naturally leads to obsolescent technologies, and it can be traumatic for workers who lose their jobs as a result. However, in the long run, creative destruction increases productivity. Job losses are part of modern capitalism, but they do not always cause permanent unemployment: for example, between 1999 and 2009, some 338.9 million private sector jobs were lost in the USA but 337.5 million new ones were created over the same period.

Joseph Schumpeter (1883–1950) was an economist who was born in modern-day Czech Republic (then part of the Austro-Hungarian Empire) and then lived in the USA after 1932. He argued that capitalism develops through innovation, which gives its developers a short-term monopoly and a period of high income (entrepreneurial profit). Schumpeter was doubtful about the future of capitalism, arguing that increasing bureaucracy would erode individual entrepreneurship. This scepticism proved to be misplaced. Neo-Schumpeterian economists adapted his theories to take account of the wider context of innovation (including companies, governments and education) in an approach called the National Innovation System.

The inventions that make our lives longer, safer, easier and more entertaining were not developed for purely altruistic reasons. In a capitalist system, innovators such as Elon Musk (b. 1971) and Steve Jobs (1955–2011) in the USA invested in new discoveries because they were reasonably certain that they would enjoy the ensuing profits. Innovation is therefore encouraged.

C

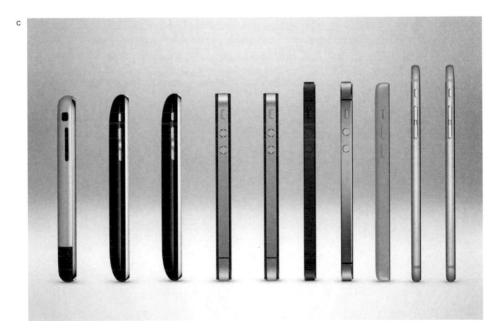

A

B

This is thanks to the patent laws and regulations that form part of the institutional framework of the capitalist system. It is not only epochal 'macro-inventions', such as the microprocessor, internal combustion engine or light bulb, that are important. 'Micro-inventions' build on existing technologies to make them more productive and efficient. They are vital to progress. These incremental innovations (for example, the iPhone has been tweaked continuously since its release in 2007, and the latest model is more than five times as powerful as the first) ensure productivity continues to grow.

As the 21st century progresses, new frontiers in biotechnology, medicine, computing, telecommunications and countless other fields will be opened up because consumers are willing to pay for them.

Liberalism emphasizes the rights of the individual. Politically, it became associated with the rise of constitutional democracy and the rule of law. No longer would royalty and the nobility dominate by right of birth. In an economic sense, liberalism ensures people can dispose of their property and pursue economic activity as they wish, thereby driving forward the capitalist system. Although there are arguments that self-interested autocrats may operate in the public interest, democracies are better for the economy. According to one MIT study, when countries move from non-democratic to democratic regimes, in the long term they experience a 20% increase in GDP per capita. Indeed, the same study found that the global shift towards democracy over the past five decades has led to a 6% increase in world GDP.

A   Virgin Galactic, founded in 2004, aims to operate regular commercial space flights, and this facility in New Mexico, USA, is its planned terminal, hangar and launch facility.
B   SpaceShipTwo (centre) is a passenger spacecraft designed for suborbital space flight. It is launched from its dual-fuselage mother ship, WhiteKnightTwo (also pictured).
C   Founded in 1976, the Cryonics Institute in Michigan, USA, preserves the bodies of its customers in liquid nitrogen after death. The hope is that the technology to revive them will be developed in the future.
D   Portraits of some of the people whose bodies have been frozen at the Cryonics Institute adorn the walls. More than 150 'people' are stored there.

Constitutional democracies are nations with fair and free elections between different political parties. Governing this system is a set of laws that enshrines the powers of government and the rights of people. These constitutions can be a formal written document (as in the USA) or an unwritten set of laws and customs (as in Britain).

Self-interested autocrats, once they are established in power, can act as 'the other invisible hand' and encourage economic growth, according to the US economist Mancur Olson (1932–98). This is because their self-interested desire to extract long-term income will lead to actions that aim to preserve and increase the wealth of the country where they hold power.

Democracies tend to be more stable and less corrupt, too, and therefore encourage long-term investment from other countries. Unlike socialist planned economies, the state tries not to intervene too much. This is not to say that the state does not have a key role. The institutionalist school of economics stresses the importance of institutions such as the state to capitalism. Among other things, the state keeps order, protects intellectual property, maintains infrastructure and protects domestic industry through foreign policy. A free market economy is the most effective system when it comes to delivering economic growth.

In a sense, the USA's rise to become the world's greatest economic power is the story of the triumph of liberalism. According to the World Bank, the USA's GDP in 2016 was $18.6 trillion, nearly two-thirds more than its nearest rival, China ($11.2 trillion), which has triple the population.

A   US President Ronald Reagan and British Prime Minister Margaret Thatcher take Lucky, one of the presidential dogs, for a walk on the White House Lawn in 1985. The two leaders were the twin standard-bearers of neoliberalism in the 1980s.

B   In the 1980s, dealers conducted transactions in person on the trading floor at the London International Financial Futures Exchange. Futures are a contract agreeing to buy or sell a commodity for a certain price at a later date.

B

During the 1980s, neoliberal policies became increasingly influential. The Reagan and Thatcher administrations in the USA and Britain aggressively promoted the free market via deregulation, privatization and tax cuts. They argued that if the state intervened in the economy, it would create more problems than it solved. By the 1990s, neoliberal policies had spread worldwide.

This certainly enriched millions of people, but the financial crisis of 2008 revealed the perils of unfettered neoliberalism. Post-crisis, political leaders must work to reform capitalism so economies return to stability.

The **institutionalist school** emphasizes the role of historical and social influences on individual economic behaviour. The main originator of the school was the Norwegian-American sociologist and economist Thorstein Veblen (1857–1929). Neo-institutional economics, which became influential during the 1980s, concentrate less on the individual and more on the impact that institutions have on the economy.

Intellectual property is a unique concept, idea or creation that is assigned to an individual or organization. It prevents others copying or profiting from this piece of work.

Free market is a system in which the economy will essentially be self-regulating, as opposed to one in which the government works to regulate economic activity. Proponents of the free market argue that bars to free trade should be removed.

Reagan and Thatcher's **neoliberal policies** were inspired by supply-side economics. This suggests that tax cuts and reducing regulations will lead to an increased supply of goods and services at lower prices, which will reduce unemployment.

СПАСИБО ЛЮБИМОМУ СТАЛИНУ –

ЗА СЧАСТЛИВОЕ ДЕТСТВО!

However, there is no need to throw out the capitalist baby with the neoliberal bathwater. The alternative is worse.

In 1917 the Russian Revolution led to the creation of the USSR. Its economic system was diametrically opposed to capitalism. Private ownership of the means of production (factories, machinery, farms and so forth) was swept away. Production was not geared to profit, but to the demands of the state. At first the 'New Economic Policy' retained some elements of capitalism and a free market (subject to state control), but this policy was abolished in 1928 when the Soviet regime attempted to invigorate the economy through the First Five-Year Plan (1928–32). This was the main economic aspect of Joseph Stalin's policy 'Socialism in One Country', which aimed to strengthen the USSR internally.

A   Created during Stalin's 'reign of terror', this Soviet propaganda poster by Viktor Govorkov (1936) states: 'Thank you beloved Stalin for our happy childhood.'
B   The famine in Ukraine in 1932-33, during which millions starved to death, was deliberately engineered by Soviet authorities to bring the region more closely under central authority.

In order to protect the nation from foreign invasion, Stalin sought to industrialize as quickly as possible. The Five-Year Plan demanded that national income double and that investment treble. All resources were focused on heavy industry: Stalin called for a 110% increase in coal production, a 200% increase in iron production and a 335% increase in electrical generation. Unrealistic production goals were set for factories, which meant that quotas could never be met. Agriculture was collectivized; individual farms were aggregated in an attempt to increase productivity and to allow workers to move away from rural areas. The Plan partly succeeded – the USSR was indeed industrialized and survived World War II – but it was highly damaging in other respects. It used forced labour from prisoners, and strikers or perceived shirkers were shot or sent to *gulags* (forced labour camps). Most detrimentally, collectivization disrupted food supply and contributed to a famine from 1932 to 1933 that killed approximately seven million people.

Joseph Stalin
(1878–1953)
led the USSR
after the death
of its first leader,
Vladimir Lenin
(1870–1924).
Stalinist economic
policy was aimed
at eradicating
every aspect
of capitalism.

The USSR enjoyed its greatest period of economic growth after World War II, when GDP per capita grew by 3.6% between 1950 and 1973. However, this relied on increasing the input of capital goods and raw materials, which was not sustainable. Between 1974 and 1984, the Soviet economy stagnated, and after 1985 it began to contract.

A Soviet stamps were issued in 1988 to mark Gorbachev's *perestroika* reforms. They were part of his wider policy of *glasnost* (openness), which sought to promote transparency within the government.

B Remnants of a statue of Stalin are wheeled away in Budapest, Hungary, in 1990. After the collapse of the USSR and the Eastern Bloc, formerly communist republics gained political independence and began to enact free market reforms and to embrace capitalism.

Mikhail Gorbachev (b. 1931) was the last leader of the USSR. After becoming head of state in 1988, he enacted a series of economic and political reforms. These contributed to the disintegration of the Soviet Union in 1991.

According to the US economists William Easterly (b. 1957) and Stanley Fischer (b. 1943), Soviet economic performance from 1960 to 1989 was the worst in the world, and it showed no signs of improvement.

The sclerotic Soviet bureaucracy, ineffective financial institutions and lack of any domestic consumer market stifled growth and prevented innovation. State-imposed output goals did not provide any incentive to improve, because increased output would only lead to raised targets.

Bonuses for good economic performance were paid monthly, which led to short-term thinking.

The only sectors in which the USSR innovated were the military and aerospace, neither of which contributed greatly to economic growth. As a result, Soviet productivity lagged behind the West and the emerging economies of East Asia. The heavy burden of defence spending, exacerbated by the costly and unsuccessful intervention in Afghanistan (1979–89), also contributed to the poor economic performance.

Mikhail Gorbachev attempted to solve this situation by liberalizing the economy in 1985, as part of his policy of *perestroika* (restructuring). Private ownership of business was encouraged and foreign investment was allowed. But it was too little too late.

B

For consumers, even purchasing basic necessities such as food and clothing became increasingly problematic; indeed, the largest and most populous of the Soviet Republics, Russia, was reliant on imports just to reach subsistence level. The USSR collapsed in 1991. In the aftermath, its former communist states in Eastern and Central Europe rushed to embrace capitalism.

Communist states were unable to keep pace with the economies of capitalist ones. Furthermore, communism had a long-term negative impact on happiness and life satisfaction: subjective well-being in ex-communist states tends to be low, even though their GDPs per capita have increased.

A

Subjective well-being is how people judge the quality of their own lives. It is usually correlated with health and wealth, although social and local contexts are also important.

A The 105-storey Ryugyong Hotel rises above Pyongyang, North Korea. Its construction began in 1987, but stalled due to lack of funding. As of 2017, the hotel remains the world's largest unoccupied building.

B These maps from 1992 and 2008 depict light pollution in the Korean Peninsula. The majority of communist North Korea has barely altered, which shows a lack of economic development. By contrast, capitalist South Korea has changed rapidly, with the area around Seoul and Incheon undergoing significant development.

1992

2008

Digital Number

High : 63

Low : 0

0 25 50 100 km

B

The Korean Peninsula provides a stark example of the benefits of capitalism and the perils of communism. After World War II, it was divided into two countries, and when communist North Korea invaded South Korea in 1950 a US-led United Nations (UN) force intervened to protect its own integrity. Since the end of the Korean War in 1953, the two Koreas have followed profoundly different paths.

In a single generation South Korea, which embraced capitalism, transformed from one of the poorest countries in the world to the 11th largest economy in the world, home to electronic giants such as Samsung (the 15th largest company in the world). South Koreans live a decade longer than their neighbours in the north (in 2015 the life expectancies of the two states were 82 and 70 years of age), and in terms of GDP per capita as of 2016 they are 40 times wealthier.

Meanwhile, communist North Korea remains relatively poor and undeveloped, with many of its citizens facing starvation. From 1994 to 1998, an economic crisis in North Korea led to the deaths of more than 300,000 people. At the same time, the 'Dear Leader' Kim Jong-il (1941–2011) was spending $800,000 a year on cognac alone. Famine was abated by the UN's World Food Programme. Ironically, capitalist South Korea and the USA provided nearly half of the humanitarian aid.

In Europe the divergent paths of East and West Germany after 1945 highlight the same point. The East German economy was centrally planned, like that of the USSR. By 1960 85% of its land had been collectivized, and the country was deeply indebted to others. By contrast, West Germany enjoyed the *Wirtschaftswunder* (economic miracle). Its 'social market economy' tempered free market ideals (such as lifting price controls and lowering taxes) with policies that protected workers by providing ample social security and pensions. When the two Germanys unified in 1991, the West's GDP per capita was double that of the East's.

A Lengthy waits for basic commodities became a common feature of East German life, as seen in this photograph (c. 1986–90) of a queue outside a butcher's shop in East Berlin.
B Across the Wall in capitalist West Berlin, food was not in short supply. The famed Café Kranzler (seen here in 1963), rebuilt after the destruction of World War II, symbolized the affluence and choice available to West Berliners.
C The Port of Shanghai is a deep-water sea port and a river port. In 2010 it overtook Singapore as the busiest container port in the world, and in 2016 it handled more than 500 million tons of cargo.

c

Even now, a quarter of a century after reunification, the average net worth of the economic assets of a household in East Germany is worth less than half of the average in West Germany. The long-term negative impacts of communism are still felt.

International trade has been part of the global economy for centuries. However, the 20th century saw a major shift. Combined with developments in transport and communications, long-distance trade became more important than ever. The main tool of this global system is the steel shipping container. Containerization enabled nations to trade with other countries where previously high transport costs made their goods prohibitively expensive.

Containerization is the process in which goods are shipped in steel containers of standardized dimensions (usually 20 or 40 feet long), which can be mechanically moved by cranes and forklifts. These containers are 'intermodal', which means they can be easily transferred between modes of transport (ships, trains and trucks). Before containerization, goods were shipped as 'break bulk cargo', which meant they had to be loaded and unloaded individually and sorted manually at dockside. This was a laborious and time-consuming process. It increased transit times because ships had to spend longer in port. Container shipping became important during the 1950s and 1960s. Since 1968 the capacity of container ships has increased by 1,200%, and the vessels are responsible for 90% of goods shipped worldwide. It is not an exaggeration to say that without containerization modern capitalism would be impossible.

This created an international market that not only lowered prices for consumers but also offered them greater choice. In particular, states such as China and India reformed and liberalized their economic policies, which gradually opened them up to capitalism. Standards of living have increased rapidly in those countries since this occurred. Integrating markets on an international scale, therefore, has the power to benefit us all. Trade agreements mean that different economies become more integrated. In 1993 a single market was created in the EU with free movement of goods, services, people and money. One year later, the North American Free Trade Agreement was signed between Mexico, Canada and the USA. Since then, trade between the three countries has quadrupled.

An ambitious proposal to reduce trade barriers between 12 Pacific Rim nations, the Trans-Pacific Partnership (TPP), was finalized in 2016. Despite the fact that the World Bank found it would have a net positive impact on all countries involved, US President Donald Trump (b. 1946) withdrew the USA from the agreement on 23 January 2017 as part of his policy of protecting the US economy. Trump will also withdraw the USA from the Transatlantic Trade and Investment Partnership, a similar trade deal that is being negotiated with the EU.

This policy is dangerously short-sighted. US manufacturing (e.g. textiles) in low-tech sectors may receive a temporary boost, but this will mean that high-tech industries and services (e.g. pharmacology and IT, in which the USA has a huge advantage and highly innovative companies) will find it more difficult to access the burgeoning economies of East Asia and South America. Furthermore, Trump is abrogating US economic leadership in the Pacific region, thereby allowing China to become more influential.

A   Globalization is often associated with 'Americanization', or the exporting of US brands and consumer goods. US fast-food restaurants such as McDonald's and KFC are now common sights throughout the world, including in China.
B   Activists at a demonstration in Santiago, Chile, in 2016 protest against the TPP and the activities of Monsanto Company, which is one of the leading manufacturers of genetically modified organisms.

Single market On 1 January 1993, the European single market was established. It aimed to promote the integration of the member states of the EU in addition to Iceland, Lichtenstein, Norway and Switzerland. Within the single market, there is free movement of goods, capital, services and people.

The **North American Free Trade Agreement** was established on 1 January 1994 between the USA, Mexico and Canada. It aimed to reduce economic barriers and to facilitate trade between the three nations.

The **Trans-Pacific Partnership** was first negotiated in 2008, with the final proposal being signed in Auckland in 2016. The nations involved were: Australia, Brunei, Canada, Chile, Japan, Malaysia, Mexico, New Zealand, Peru, Singapore, the USA and Vietnam. Together they accounted for around 40% of world GDP. Negotiations are currently being pursued on an alternative trade agreement, the Regional Comprehensive Economic Partnership, which will not involve the USA, Canada, Mexico, Peru and Chile. This new agreement will be widened to also include Cambodia, China, India, Indonesia, Laos, Myanmar, Philippines, South Korea and Thailand.

B

A

Cristina Fernández de Kirchner (b. 1953) was president of Argentina from 2007 to 2015. Her left-wing populist policies stressed the defence and extension of civil rights. Economically, she aimed to encourage the development of Argentina's economy by promoting domestic industry.

Globalization is used frequently as a stick with which to beat the capitalism system, with critics in the West arguing that it will destroy jobs and limit growth. The actual situation is more complex. Local economies are able to shape their own destinies. Globalization cannot help an economy if it is not productive and efficient. Furthermore, not all sectors are subject to globalization. Occupations that can be automated may be relocated overseas, but services such as housing, medicine and education mostly remain rooted because it is impossible to move them. The most important sector in global trade is manufacturing, but even within manufacturing not all parts of the business are subject to globalization. For example, the majority of Nike products are manufactured in factories in Asia, but the design, marketing and distribution of goods still needs to be done locally.

A   Thai factory workers labour on a production line in 1997, making Nike shoes at a plant owned by the Saha Union company in Bangkok.

B   Labourers work at a garment factory in Bac Giang province, near Hanoi in 2015. According to the World Bank, Vietnam would potentially have benefited the most of all the countries in the TPP in terms of GDP growth and exports.

Globalization helps countries play to their strengths. This special-ization reduces prices. When political leaders try to reverse globalization, it can be disastrous for the consumer.

In 2009 the Argentinian president Cristina Fernández de Kirchner imposed a 50% import tax on foreign goods and passed a law requiring electronic companies to assemble their products in Argentina. Apple refused and withdrew from the country. It became cheaper to fly to the USA to buy an iPhone than to purchase one in Argentina. Initially, phones produced by companies who complied with the new law, such as BlackBerry, were comparatively outdated and expensive. Furthermore, the law created an underground economy in smart-phones. Of the 12 million purchased in Argentina in 2016, 15% were bought through the black market. In 2017 restrictions on Apple were lifted in Argentina, although it still faces a high import tax that makes its smartphones 25% more expensive than locally assembled models.

Think about all of the objects you own and take away all of the items that were manufactured in another continent. How much would be left in your home?

B

3. Capitalism in Crisis

A

In the drive to make as much money as possible, as quickly as possible, bankers and financiers have dangerously destabilized the world economy.

One of the bywords of the recent history of capitalism is financialization. This is the process by which any and every thing can be translated into tradable financial assets, mostly in the form of securities. Some people argue that financialization does not create actual products but is essentially an attempt to make money out of money. It does not really contribute to long-term economic growth; it merely enriches financial institutions.

This process was one of the main causes of the global financial crisis in 2008, the worst since the Wall Street Crash in 1929 (see Chapter 1). The early 21st century saw a long period of low interest, which led to a 'credit boom', as lending by banks rapidly expanded. In the quest for profit, US banks lent billions of dollars to subprime borrowers to buy homes, knowing that they would be unlikely to pay back the loans on time. By 2006 some 20% of US residential mortgages were subprime.

Securities are, broadly speaking, tradable financial assets (although their exact definition varies by country). Banks and investors favour them because they can be liquidated easily. There are two types: debt securities (purchased from a body that then owes the investor debt, which generally must be repaid with interest, e.g. a bond) and equity securities (an ownership stake, such as a stock). Almost anything can be turned into a security; in 1997 David Bowie issued a $55 million debt security in the form of a ten-year bond against the value of the current and future revenues from his pre-1990 back catalogue.

The **global financial crisis in 2008** threatened numerous financial institutions. Many governments bailed out banks but they could not prevent a decline in the stock markets. Markets began to stabilize in 2009 but the effects of the crisis are still being felt. This has been the most serious financial crisis since the 1930s.

Subprime borrowers are people who are deemed to be high risk because they are potentially unlikely to pay back their loan to schedule. As such, they face higher interest rates and less favourable terms of loan than other individuals.

B

A Seen here on his speedboat in the Caribbean in the 1990s, Jordan Belfort (right) was a stockbroker who won fortune and infamy as the 'Wolf of Wall Street'. He made millions of dollars by defrauding his clients, and his life was the subject of a 2013 film directed by Martin Scorsese.

B Crowds gather on Wall Street, New York, after the stock market crashed in 1929. The event presaged the Great Depression, which lasted for 12 years.

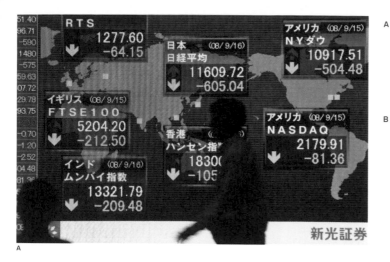

A   This board indicates the massive drop in global financial markets after news of the closure and bankruptcy of Lehman Brothers broke in September 2008. It was the largest firm to ever file for bankruptcy in the USA.

B   Mass foreclosures occurred across the USA in 2008. During the subprime mortgage crisis, millions of people were unable to make their repayments and were forced to sell their properties at a loss.

Without the knowledge of the borrowers, more than 80% of these subprime mortgages were packaged into tradable assets called collaterized debt obligations (CDOs). CDOs are bundles of different types of debt, both safe and risky. They are tremendously complex (most require 30,000 pages of documentation), which makes due diligence near-impossible. Rating agencies deemed these CDOs to be highly trustworthy and awarded them the highest triple-A rating. Investors worldwide rushed to purchase CDOs without realizing how many high-risk loans they contained. They protected themselves against the risk of default through credit default swaps (CDSs), which insurers believed they would barely ever have to pay out.

Almost everyone saw CDOs as a reliable investment because of the strength of the US housing market. But an over-reliance on property dangerously unbalanced the economy, with three-quarters of GDP related to housing. Attracted by low interest rates, many US homeowners borrowed against the value of their homes. These equity withdrawals hit an annual high of $975 billion (7% of GDP) before the crash, thereby loading the system with even more debt.

When the value of US real estate began to fall, it threw the financial system into chaos as it became clear that the debts would never be repaid. By 2009 some 15 million homes in the USA had mortgages worth more than the value of the house itself. It also became clear that the entire edifice was built on quicksand and that the CDOs were worthless. The ensuing panic caused two major investment banks, Bear Stearns and Lehman Brothers, to collapse.

The financial crisis spread worldwide. 2008 saw record falls in share prices from New York (34%) to Paris (43%) to Shanghai (65%). The IMF reported that from 2007 to 2010 financial institutions reduced the value of US-originated assets by $2.7 trillion. In addition, trust in the economy collapsed, which meant that no one was willing to lend money to stimulate growth. Job losses followed: 240 million worldwide. Millions of people had their homes repossessed or found their savings had been wiped out (British savers lost £5 billion as a result of the crisis). Since then, real wages have fallen or stagnated in Japan, the USA and Britain. However, the wealthy were able to insulate themselves from this crisis.

The vast majority of financial institutions saw 2008 as a black swan event. In fact, the crisis was the inevitable product of the recent evolution of the financial industry. Modern financial practices increased the chances of disaster at the same time as exacerbating the damage.

Financial crises are a dangerously familiar part of the economy. They have occurred since the early days of capitalism, from the Tulip mania of 1637 to the South Sea bubble of 1719–20. Banks and governments should know better.

From 1970 to 2007, there were 124 systemic banking crises in 101 countries, and 19 countries experienced them more than once. In some countries, they were endemic (there were four in Argentina, for example). So how did we get to this point? The crisis of 2008 was symptomatic of the recklessness of the banking industry. In a series of neoliberal-inspired reforms stretching back to the 1980s banks worldwide were deregulated, which allowed them to pursue increasingly risky money-making schemes. This process was most revolutionary in the USA.

A

A   *Satire on Tulip Mania* (c. 1640) by Jan Brueghel the Younger lampooned the recent speculation in rare tulips by depicting dealers and customers as foolish, brainless monkeys dressed in human clothes.

B   Argentina was in economic depression from 1998 until 2002. In December 2001, there were protests, civil unrest and rioting against the government's failure to address the ongoing financial crisis.

B

Tulip mania Tulips were introduced to Western Europe from Asia during the later 16th century. They became particularly popular in the Dutch Republic, where their price rose rapidly. Investors traded futures (contracts that gave their holders the right to purchase tulip bulbs at a certain price at a specified date in the future), with some changing hands ten times in one day. The bubble burst in February 1637 when demand suddenly crashed.

South Sea bubble
The South Sea Company was founded in London in 1711 and given a monopoly on trade with South America. However, it was unable to conduct much business in South America because Spain dominated the region. In January 1720, in order to raise prices of South Sea Company shares, the company's directors circulated claims that profits were rising. This caused a frenzy of demand. Despite the company's poor performance, in six months the value of shares rose from £128 to £1,050. It became clear that the value of shares was widely inflated, and the rush to sell them brought their value down to £175 by September. Even the great scientist Sir Isaac Newton was unable to resist the lure of a quick profit; he lost £20,000 (worth about £3 million today) when the bubble burst.

Until the 1970s, US banking had been highly regulated. The most important piece of legislation was the Glass-Steagall Act of 1933, which separated the activities of commercial and investment banks. Only the former could take deposits and only the latter could underwrite securities. This protected savers, because it meant that their banks could not put their deposits at risk by investing them in securities. The Gramm-Leach-Bliley Act of 1999 removed this barrier and allowed the consolidation of the different types of bank (and insurance brokers) into single financial holding companies. This led to a rush of mergers and acquisitions as commercial banks acquired investment banks. For example, Chase Manhattan merged with JP Morgan in 2000, and banks such as Morgan Stanley and Goldman Sachs, which had previously been investment banks, began to operate additionally as commercial banks. There was no regulatory oversight.

A **black swan** is an event perceived to have been impossible to predict, and beyond the expected probabilities built into statistical models. The term originates from the Western assumption that black swans were non-existent, which was proved false when Europeans discovered the species in Australia. The developer of the theory is Nassim Nicholas Taleb (b. 1960), a Lebanese-American finance professor and former trader.

A

Deregulation allowed bankers to put profits before investor security and the results were disastrous.

The island nation of Iceland (population *c.* 334,000) provides the most vivid example of the risks of deregulation. In 2001 its financial sector was deregulated. Icelandic banks expanded aggressively on the world market by offering savers (particularly Dutch and British) high rates of interest. Their foreign debt reached around $112 billion (seven times Iceland's GDP). When the crisis hit in 2008, trust in Iceland's banks failed and the three largest (Glitnir, Kaupthing and Landsbanki) were put into receivership. The collapse plunged Iceland into chaos: its stock exchange fell by 90% and unemployment rates nearly trebled. As a result, Iceland became the first developed country in 30 years to request an IMF bailout. It took until 2011 for its economy to resume growth.

Shareholder value is a proposition that the best way to determine a company's success is through its performance in the stock market, both in terms of value per share and dividends paid out.

A   The evolution of the trading floor at the New York Stock Exchange (top to bottom) in the 1940s, the 1970s and 2011. Trading has become increasingly computerized, allowing transactions to be conducted almost instantaneously.

B   Protesters burn an effigy of the Icelandic Prime Minister Geir Haarde during a demonstration in 2009 over the handling of the financial crisis in Reykjavik. He resigned as leader shortly afterwards.

Short-termism is endemic to modern banking. Most financial institutions are publicly tradable companies, which makes them more accountable to their shareholders than to their depositors. In the rush to achieve shareholder value, banks pursue activities that are inimical to long-term stability. The payment of bonuses encourages bank employees to take on more risk so they can maximize their annual payout. But individual risk-taking can lead to banks suffering huge losses.

B

The largest trading loss in history occurred from 2007 to 2008 when a US bond trader called Howie Hubler lost Morgan Stanley $9 billion as a result of investments in CDOs and CDSs. It is common for bankers to take on more risk than is healthy because there is huge pressure to not hold back. Technology has made buying and selling securities easier and quicker, but it has also made banking riskier. 'Fat-finger errors' are common. They occur when a trader presses the wrong number when making a trade.

In 2001 a Lehman Brothers trader in London wiped £30 billion off FTSE by making sell orders 100 times too big. The same year, a UBS trader in Tokyo sold 610,000 shares for ¥16 when the price should have been ¥420,000. Computerization means that such orders are very hard to cancel. In recent years, banks have increasingly automated their practices by putting more faith in high-frequency trading, which brings its own potential volatility in the form of 'flash crashes'. These are rapid short-term declines in the value of securities where billions can be lost rapidly. For example, on 6 May 2010 US markets fell 5% in only 20 minutes.

FTSE The Financial Times Stock Exchange Index measures the value of the top 100 companies on the London Stock Exchange in terms of market capitalization (the value of their shares). It began in 1984 with a base value of 1,000. Its highest value to date is 7,460 on 17 May 2017.

High-frequency trading uses algorithms (algobots) and other techniques to rapidly buy and sell securities with the aim of taking instant advantage of changing conditions. Such is the value of saving time that in 2010 Spread Networks unveiled a new fibre-optic cable between Chicago and New York. Its cost was $300 million; time saved was three milliseconds.

After 2008, rather than punishing banks or imposing radical reforms, most governments worked to save them. Banks were bailed out and debts were written off or purchased by the state. Under the Troubled Asset Relief Program of 2010, the US government authorized $700 billion to stabilize banks. In Britain, £50 million was spent purchasing shares in banks to prop them up. Even the oldest surviving bank in the world, Italy's Banca Monte dei Paschi di Siena (founded in 1472), built up huge losses investing in risky financial products. As a result, the Italian government had to spend more than €4 billion rescuing the bank in 2016.

A   Shepard Fairey's Barack Obama 'Hope' poster of 2008 was adapted for the 2011 Occupy movement, which protested against global social and economic inequality.

B   The 'Rise Up' poster was designed by Nathan Mandreza for the 2011 Occupy Wall Street protests, which gave the movement worldwide recognition.

C   'Monopoly Tower' by Lalo Alcaraz features Occupy's slogan, 'We are the 99%', which draws attention to the huge disparities that exist in status and income, with wealth and power concentrated in the top 1%.

D   'Occupy Wall Street' (silkscreen on paper) designed by Jeanne Verdoux, 2011. The movement soon spread to the financial districts of cities across the world.

CHAPTER 3

Bankers are free to engage in risky behaviour because they know they will be bailed out and that harsh punishment is unlikely. Only one banker has been imprisoned as a result of their actions leading up to the 2008 crisis: in 2013 Kareem Serageldin of Credit Suisse was sentenced to 30 months for fraud. Fines, which are usually tax-deductible, were levied against corporations but not individual bankers.

Emmanuel Macron (b. 1977) is a French politician who was Minister of Economy, Industry and Digital Affairs from 2014 to 2016. A former member of the Socialist Party, he founded a new centrist party called En Marche! and was elected president of France in the 2017 elections. Macron won 24% of the vote in the first round. In the second round, he triumphed over his far-right opponent Marine Le Pen of the National Front.

John Key (b. 1961) was prime minister of New Zealand for the centre-right National Party from 2008 to 2016.

Part of the problem is that big banks are entrenched in the top levels of government. The finance sector lobbies governments aggressively for favourable treatment. In the last US election cycle (2015–16), $2.8 billion was spent on lobbying. It is no surprise, therefore, that lucrative employment in finance is a common destination for many politicians when they leave office. In 2017 George Osborne, the former British Chancellor of the Exchequer, became an 'adviser' to BlackRock, the world's largest investment firm, which manages funds worth more than £4 trillion. Conversely, former bankers frequently occupy high political office worldwide: French president Emmanuel Macron was an investment banker at the French branch of the Rothschild Group and former prime minister of New Zealand John Key was head of global foreign exchange at Merrill Lynch for six years.

C

D

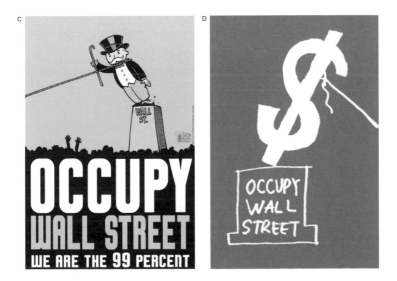

Lessons have not been learnt. Despite the global financial crisis of 2008, banks continue to lend at record rates – more than $60 trillion since 2008. Global debt is around three times higher than global GDP. While the world struggles to recover from 2008, the seeds for another crisis have already been sown.

Meanwhile, the architects of the past crisis remain wealthy and secure, with governments passing on the cost to society at large through severe austerity policies. Capitalism is a competitive system. Inherently, there will always be winners (the rich) and losers (the poor).

A

A   On 21 June 2017, protesters demonstrated in London against the government's handling of the fire at Grenfell Tower, which killed at least 71 people.
B   Although Grenfell Tower is in one of London's most affluent areas, the block contained public housing flats. The disaster became symbolic of how austerity policies have damaged working-class communities.

B

Its proponents argue that upward mobility is possible, and that inequality will in fact encourage people to work harder to enrich themselves.

Neoliberal policies have meant that income inequality has increased in most countries since the 1980s. Far from bringing wealth to all, capitalism has led to an increasing division in society between rich and poor. In 1965 the average US chief executive earned 24 times more than the average production worker. Now they make around 200 times more.

Austerity policies occur when governments want to reduce their deficits quickly so their revenues do not outpace their expenditure. As part of this effort, public spending is cut and taxes are increased, or both. In 2008 many European countries adopted such policies.

Thomas Piketty (b. 1971) is a professor at L'École des hautes études en sciences sociales, where he concentrates his research on inequality of wealth. He argues that this inequality will progressively increase over time because the rate of economic growth in developed countries is lower than the return on capital invested.

In 2013 the French economist Thomas Piketty published *Capital in the Twenty-First Century*, which argued that economic inequality is on the rise, with no end in sight unless governments forcibly redistribute income. Even in developing economies such as China, India and South Africa, more and more income has been accumulating among the wealthiest.

Worldwide, individuals who are worth more than $1 million make up 0.334% of the world population but control 33.2% of global wealth.

Financial inequality is now at levels unknown since the 19th century. Furthermore, in the USA the top 0.1% are now worth as much as the combined total of the bottom 90%, and this trend can also be seen across the West. Clearly, wealth insulated the established elite from the impact of the crisis in 2008.

The young in particular have been cut out of economic growth, and for the first time in history they will probably not reach the levels of wealth enjoyed by their parents.

C

In recent years, youth unemployment has rocketed in Europe. Economic integration has not helped, because membership of the Eurozone means that these countries cannot decrease the value of their currency, which would stimulate exports. As a result, in 2017 Greek and Spanish youth unemployment was 48% and 40.5%, respectively. In France about one-quarter of those under the age of 25 who want a job do not have one. This has led to a surge in support for far-right parties such as the National Front (which won 21.3% of the vote in the first round and one-third in the second round of the French presidential election in 2017).

A The July 2015 cover of French magazine *Marianne* satirizes the German Chancellor, Angela Merkel, who was criticized for her harsh handling of the Greek government's debt crisis.

B The March 2015 cover of German magazine *Der Spiegel* juxtaposes Merkel with a group of Nazi officers in Greece. The headline reads, 'How Europeans look at the Germans – The German Superiority'.

C This graffiti on the Bank of Greece in Athens reads, 'Here are the Thieves'. On 20 May 2010, some 25,000 people marched through Athens to protest against the austerity cuts implemented as a result of the country's crippling debts.

Research by the German economists Markus Brückner (b. 1983) and Hans Peter Grüner (b. 1966) found that in countries with high levels of inequality, decrease in growth is associated with an increase in support for right-wing or nationalist parties and policies, as people search for radical solutions to their gloomy economic futures.

The elite enjoy the highest incomes and have the resources to pay teams of lawyers and accountants to screen them from state taxation. Their wealth allows them to lobby governments to pass policies that favour them, such as tax cuts for the rich. In the USA, a Supreme Court decision in 2010 (Citizens United v. Federal Electoral Commission) declared that campaign donations are a form of free speech and are therefore protected under the Constitution. Canadian author Naomi Klein argues that over the past four decades corporate interests used crises (such as the invasion of Iraq in 2003) to push through policies that benefit the elite, as well as to excuse the erosion of civil liberties and the violation of human rights.

Declining tax rates and creative accounting allow the wealthiest to earn more and to save more.

Naomi Klein (b. 1970) is a Canadian author and activist who is one of the foremost critics of globalization and capitalism.

A   *Eclipse*, the luxury yacht owned by the Russian oligarch Roman Abramovich, cost around $500 million and has two helicopter pads, two swimming pools and a missile detection system.

B   A protest against Uber took place in Paris in 2016. Critics of the ride-sharing company argue that it ignores safety and licensing laws, breaches customer privacy and avoids paying taxes.

C   Most of the couriers for Deliveroo, an online food ordering service founded in 2013, are self-employed. They are part of the growing 'gig economy' in which employment is on a short-term basis.

A

B

C

This wealth does not 'trickle down' to the poorest people in society, whose wages cannot keep pace with the resources that the wealthy control. Instead, it remains concentrated in the hands of the most privileged people in society.

Free market economies strive to maximize profits and productivity through 'creative destruction'. In order to progress, old technologies and industries are swept away regardless of the cost to people's livelihoods. Indeed, automation threatens to make millions unemployed. A study in 2013 found that 47% of US workers were in occupations that had a high risk of automation (leading to unemployment). The danger is that many of these people will be left with part-time, low-paid jobs in the service sector that offer neither satisfaction nor security. Furthermore, in the globalized economy, if international corporations can shift operations to a country with lower wages or lower production costs, they will.

A

Only the elite will benefit from this. Across the West, towns
and regions that were once devoted to industries such
as coal mining, ship building or textile manufacture have
suffered the loss of these businesses. The neoliberal tide
has led to the privatization of many industries; usually this
is an irreversible process that results in higher prices and
lay-offs. Corporations that were once accountable to the
people are now accountable to shareholders and driven by
profit motive. Trade unions, which previously gave workers
a voice, have become marginalized. For example, in the
USA only 11% of workers are unionized. Since its peak
in 1979, the number of British union members has halved
from over 13 million to 6.2 million in 2016. The trend has
been repeated in Germany and France, once strongholds
of union membership. Strong unions provide a voice
in support of rules and regulations that benefit workers.

Solidarity between workers
may overcome other
inequalities in society. For
example, in the USA black
workers who are unionized
earn one-third more than
those who are not.

B

A/B Floats featuring the British Prime Minister Theresa May and the US President Donald Trump, with the Statue of Liberty, took part in the annual Rose Monday Parade on 27 February 2017 in Düsseldorf, Germany. Brexit and the Trump presidency have provided rich fodder for public satire, protesting against the growing tide of nationalist populism.

In this climate in which traditional economic identities and job security have been swept away, it is little wonder that many people feel abandoned by this 'progress'. In 2016 alone, Donald Trump became president of the USA and Britain voted to leave the EU. Both developments are partly a rejection of the unequal system of capitalism that arose in the 21st century.

National sovereignty will be eroded at the expense of profit.

In the same way that capitalism created inequality within nations, it also increased global inequality. The neoliberal model espoused by influential institutions such as the IMF urges countries to deregulate and to pursue free trade policies, primarily by reducing tariffs on imports. Indeed, adopting such measures is part of the loan agreements.

Yet, in developing economies that opened up to the free market in the 1980s and 1990s, growth slowed considerably compared to the 1960s and 1970s when protectionist policies were in place. The foreign goods that flooded into these countries from more developed nations undercut domestic production, thus preventing sustained economic growth. Unsurprisingly, it is the more developed nations, who have the biggest voting power over the IMF, that have been enriched.

Ha-Joon Chang (b. 1963) is based at the University of Cambridge. He consistently challenges mainstream economic thought, with much of his opinion being expressed in his work *23 Things They Don't Tell You About Capitalism* (2010).

A   This campaign by Cordaid,
    one of the world's largest
    international development
    organizations, highlights the
    huge disparity in global wealth,
    showing how the money that
    the West spends on luxury
    goods could buy necessities
    in other parts of the world.
B   The government of the Maldives
    held an underwater cabinet
    meeting in October 2009 to
    draw attention to how global
    warming and rising sea levels
    are threatening the country's
    existence. The Maldives is the
    world's lowest-lying country,
    and faces destruction if climate
    change continues unabated.

B

The West should recognize that the free market will not make poor nations rich.

The South Korean economist Ha-Joon Chang showed that all major developed nations were highly protectionist while they were building up their economic strength; this is true of Britain from the 1720s to the 1850s and of the USA from the 1830s to the 1940s. Proponents of globalization may point to the fact that per capita incomes in the non-developed world grew 2.6% from 1980 to 2009. However, if India and China (neither of which have wholly embraced neoliberal capitalism) are excluded from the figure, then the situation looks less rosy. Latin America grew by 1.1% and Sub-Saharan Africa by only 0.2%.

A

Inequality between rich and poor nations is on the increase and roughly tripled from 1960 to 2016. Capitalism has not enriched all parts of the world equally – the gap between the developed and non-developed world has not been bridged and in fact it may be widening.

The worst of the damage caused by capitalism is yet to be revealed. Earth is warming up. This will cause sea levels to rise and lead to floods, which could drown island nations such as the Maldives and Tuvalu, while endangering coastal areas. Rising temperatures will make agriculture less productive and force up food prices. The proximate cause is the carbon released into our atmosphere through the burning of fossil fuels, which increased markedly after the Industrial Revolution. Emissions have slowed since 2000 – in the 2000s the average annual increase was 3.5% – but in the past three years they have gone up by around 0.3% a year on average.

The World Meteorological Organization reported that 2011 to 2015 was the hottest five-year period on record. By 2050 global temperatures will probably be 2.0–3.6°C (35–38°F) higher than before 1800. Despite knowing the long-term dangers of relying on oil, gas and coal, big businesses continue to depend on them. In many nations, these energy firms are too influential for the state to regulate, so they continue their damaging activity. As a result of their political influence, fossil fuel companies receive around £1 trillion a year in subsidies. To make matters worse, forests, which provide us with oxygen, are being steadily cleared, mostly to make way for cattle ranches. According to the World Wildlife Foundation, we are losing the equivalent of 48 football fields of forest every minute.

By concentrating on short-term profits, the capitalist system is endangering the future of our planet.

A   This aerial photograph, taken on 6 July 2010, shows concession areas of Indonesia's biggest palm oil firm, Sinar Mas, in Kapuas Hulu, West Kalimantan province on Borneo island. A Greenpeace report has accused the company of devastating millions of hectares of rainforest and driving endangered species into extinction.
B   The price of progress? China's increasing urbanization and industrialization come at an environmental cost. This image shows heavy smog at the Olympic Park in Beijing on 1 December 2015.

4. Adapting the Capitalist Model

A

The social, economic, political and environmental challenges of the rest of the 21st century will make the adaptation of capitalism imperative.

There are viable alternatives to traditional models of capitalism. Proponents of neoliberal capitalism argue that governments must let the free market run its course. Yet, China's astounding transformation in recent decades shows that state management of the economy is compatible with economic growth.

Deng Xiaoping (1904–97) became China's paramount leader in 1978, when he outsmarted Hua Guofeng (1921–2008), the chosen successor of the leader of the Communist Chinese Revolution Mao Zedong (1893–1976). Deng instituted a new ideology called 'Socialism with Chinese characteristics', which combined aspects of socialism with market capitalism. In 1989 Deng used force to crack down on the anti-regime student-led protests at Tiananmen Square. The same year, he resigned from some of his positions and officially retired from politics in 1992. His successor Jiang Zemin (b. 1926) maintained many of Deng's policies.

However, the Chinese government does not oversee a planned economy on the scale of the USSR. Deng Xiaoping adapted communism for local conditions. His doctrine of 'one country, two systems' allowed for the coexistence of capitalist regions, such as Hong Kong and Macau, within the socialist state.

Under the terms of the Constitution of the People's Republic of China of 1982, private enterprise was allowed, trade was liberalized and foreign investment was permitted. The government did not try to control every aspect of the economy directly. However, it still commanded control over the Chinese economy relative to other states. The Chinese state set out economic goals and regulations with the aim of ensuring sustained national growth. Large enterprises – from mining to banking to air travel – continue to be owned by the state and run in the national interest. In Fortune's 2016 list of the corporations with the largest revenues, three of the top five were Chinese and state-owned (the electric utility company State Grid Corporation of China and two oil and gas producers, China National Petroleum and Sinopec Group), with a combined revenue of $923.2 billion.

Over the past 30 years, China's economy averaged a growth rate of more than 10%, showing that slavishly following traditional capitalism is not the only path to economic development.

A   A scene from China in 1983. The poster promises great things for the country, post-Chairman Mao, with a buoyant consumer market and one-child families.
B   'Create a Great New Situation in Socialist Modernized Construction', a Chinese propaganda poster from the 1980s.
C   'Enthusiastically Celebrate the Return of Hong Kong' (1997). The boy holds the flag used after the transfer of sovereignty from Britain to China.

A

An alternative approach to capitalism is 'economic democracy', which aims to preserve capitalism's best features while controlling its excesses. A key component of this is extending democracy to the workplace. Under this system, management is not accountable to shareholders but to employees, who also share in profits. This worker-elected leadership means there is no risk of a gap in effective demand developing, because worker compensation matches any increases in productivity.

One of the main proponents of economic democracy, David Schweickart, also advocates a flat-rate tax on all revenue-generating property, such as a factory. The tax collected is proportionately and transparently reinvested into the economy, thereby causing the 'democratization of the economy'.

A   In 1987 the population of Shanghai was around 11 million. Although the city was China's main economic hub, it had not yet become a global financial centre.

B   In 1993 the Chinese government opened up Shanghai to foreign investment. Its population reached 23 million, and its new skyline symbolized China's growing economic strength.

B

Effective demand is a measure of the goods and services that consumers are willing and able (based on their income) to buy. If productivity increases at a higher rate than wages, effective demand will fall.

David Schweickart (b. 1942) is a US philosopher and mathematician, as well as a major proponent of economic democracy.

Joseph Stiglitz (b. 1943) is a US economist based at Columbia University. From 1995 to 1997, he was chairman of the US president's Council of Economic Advisers, and from 1997 to 2000, he was chief economist of the World Bank. Stiglitz is one of the most influential and cogent critics of laissez-faire economics and the process of globalization.

One of the main causes of the crisis in 2008 was the failure of the financial sector to behave responsibly. This sector's reform is central to any modification of the capitalist model. US economist Joseph Stiglitz argues that banking has two core functions: first, to provide efficient methods of payment, and second, to assess and manage risk and provide loans. These roles make banks pivotal to the economy and governments eager to bail them out. If the banking industry fails completely, bills are not paid, investments are lost and loans are not made. In short, society grinds to a halt. In the lead-up to 2008, many banks neglected their core functions in favour of increasingly speculative activities.

The potential negative consequences of bank failure are most serious in systemically important financial institutions (SIFIs). According to the Financial Stability Board, an international monitory body for global finance, in 2016 there were 30 SIFIs, with the two largest being Citigroup and JP Morgan Chase. The collapse of SIFIs would cause significant and global economic damage, but their importance creates a huge potential of moral hazard among employees and investors, who may pursue riskier activities because they believe there is an implicit safety net (i.e. the government will bail them out). Given this, it is possible that SIFIs have become larger than is healthy for the economy. A long-term solution may be to break them up into smaller bodies, although given their power and clout this is unlikely to happen.

Since 2008 governments have attempted to regulate banking. In the USA, the Dodd-Frank Act of 2010 introduced new provisions, such as requiring lenders to ensure that borrowers are solvent enough to repay home loans. An important part of this act is the Volcker Rule, which limits the ability of banks to make speculative investments that put the money of depositors at risk. In 2011 the Vickers Commission made recommendations to reform British banking. It proposed that core services (e.g. depositing) are ring-fenced from risky activities (e.g. securities trading), and that banks retain sufficient reserves of capital in case of crisis (they have until 2019 to do this). In the EU, similar new supervisions and regulations were planned for banking under the de Larosière Report of 2009 and the Liikanen Report of 2012.

A

Given the increasing interconnectedness of the economy and the fact that large banks have dozens of offshore subsidiaries, reform must be international. The Third Basel Accord was published in 2011, but pressure from banking means it will not be implemented until 2019. It aims to make banks more resistant to shocks by setting minimum levels of capital they must hold, limiting how leveraged they can be, and making them more transparent. The Accord has faced criticism from both sides: some believe it is too strict and will limit growth; others think it is too lenient and will not prevent a future crisis.

A   In retrospect, the Wall Street Crash of 1929 served as a harbinger of further crises to come in the 20th century. This photograph by Walker Evans (c. 1928–30) offers a dry comment on those tough times.

B   The collapse of Lehman Brothers investment bank on 15 September 2008 heralded a global financial crash. Corruption, theft and a rash reliance on subprime mortgage-backed securities all played their part in its downfall.

Basel Accord The Basel Committee on Banking Supervision is an international body based in Switzerland. Founded in 1974, its aim is to improve the supervision of banking. The Committee has 45 members from 28 jurisdictions. Periodically, it issues Accords, which set rules and standards for banks. The first was published in 1988 and the second in 2004.

Leverage (also known as gearing) is the use of borrowed funds to purchase an asset.

A

Over the past 50 years, banking has gone from being viewed as somewhat staid and traditional to being one of the most lucrative and dynamic industries in the world. It attracts many of the brightest and most ambitious people.

Banks hire quants with advanced degrees in physics, mathematics or engineering. Consequently, a great deal of human capital formation no longer contributes to improving long-term economic productivity through innovations, but instead is devoted to increasing the dividends of shareholders. The talent of the quants has little or no chance of producing positive externalities that will benefit wider society. Reforms that limit the salaries and bonuses paid to bankers may address this, but it is unlikely they will be implemented. For example, in 2016 Britain, France and Ireland, among others, refused to comply with EU rules that would cap banker bonuses at 100% of salary.

A   In the early 20th century, jobs in banking were seen to be somewhat
    monotonous, before glamour and prestige energized the financial sector.
B   Traders and clerks at the CME Group celebrate the final trading session
    of the year on 31 December 2010 in Chicago, Illinois. The US stock indices
    posted positive returns for 2010 with the S&P, Dow and Nasdaq on pace
    to close the year up more than 10%.

B

Although inadequate, at least some regulation has been put in place to prevent further crises. In the future, governments must remain assiduous to ensure that regulations are enforced and also adapted for changing conditions.

Consumers have a role to play, too. It is essential that they are familiar with the terms and conditions of financial products. Although reading the small print is wearisome, it is vital to know exactly what kind of agreement is being entered into, and the risks involved.

Quant is an abbreviation of quantitative analyst. A quant specializes in using mathematical and statistical techniques to analyse financial markets.

Human capital formation Human capital is the knowledge, values, skills and experiences that can be harnessed to perform labour that produces goods and services. The main component of how human capital is formed is education and training. However, it can also extend to other areas such as health, because it maintains human capital. The Nobel Prize-winning US economist Gary Becker (1930-2014) argued that effective human capital formation was a vital component in achieving significant economic growth.

A

B

Consumers must also be aware of promises that are 'too good to be true'. They should remember the efficient-market hypothesis of US economist Eugene Fama, which suggests that investors cannot consistently generate returns beyond the average market rate.

In the long-term, 'beating the market' is unlikely.

Over the past three decades, inequality has increased in the developed world. Even if you are a proponent of free-market capitalism, this is still a problem-atic development that could have long-term economic costs.

The creation of a wealthy over-class prevents upward social mobility. In countries where inequality is high – Britain and the USA, for example – intergenerational income mobility (the extent that incomes change across generations) tends to be low.

This is a symptom of a closed system in which talented individuals from outside of wealthy families are unable to fulfil their potential.

A highly unbalanced distribution of wealth has a deleterious impact on general demand. Overall consumption levels depend far more on catering to a mass market than to an elite one – goods and services from the CLEWI cannot sustain an economy. In addition, inequality narrows the taxation base of governments by creating an under-class that does not earn enough to pay income tax. This means that governments become less able to finance vital areas such as infrastructure and welfare.

Inequality also leads to increasing disillusion with political systems. In itself, a crisis of democracy is disastrous, but it has economic implications, too. The development of capitalism and its positive effects often go hand-in-hand with representative democracy.

Eugene Fama (b. 1939) is a Nobel Prize-winning economist, best known for his analysis of stock prices. His work shows that they are near-impossible to predict in the short-term because new information is rapidly incorporated in the price of stocks.

CLEWI For the past 40 years, Forbes has calculated the Cost of Living Extremely Well Index (CLEWI) using a bundle of 40 items, including yachts, opera tickets, thoroughbred horses, furs, champagne and cosmetic surgery.

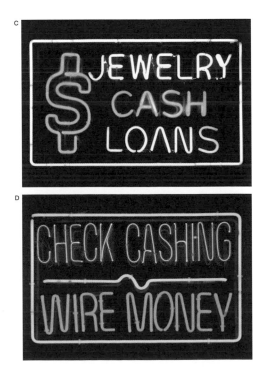

C

D

A–D   Neon signs advertise various short-term money-lending services. These 'payday loans' are generally for small amounts of money, which are supposed to be repaid when the customer receives their salary. In many areas, this sector is very lightly regulated, and the annual percentage rate of interest for these loans can be more than 1,000%. If the loans are not repaid promptly, they can leave people suffering under mounting debts.

A

In most developed nations, the citizens overthrew hereditary elites to create a society in which political power and wealth were more broadly distributed. Over time democracy deepened to include women and minority groups. When more people hold governments responsible, it leads to the creation of inclusive institutions that allow more of the population to take advantage of economic opportunities.

But there is a significant risk that those with the lowest income will essentially disenfranchise themselves through apathy. This means that elites could have unfettered dominance of government, operated entirely to their benefit without any regard for ensuring and extending prosperity and security throughout society. If a major crisis occurs, there is no reason to expect that the wealthiest individuals will stick around to help the recovery.

Some of the super-wealthy are so pessimistic about the world's future that they have made elaborate plans to protect themselves in the event of social breakdown, investing in bunkers and gold bullion. New Zealand is seen as the ultimate bolt-hole: for example, Peter Thiel (b. 1967), the billionaire cofounder of PayPal, has invested millions of dollars there.

Redistribution of wealth would ensure that inequality does not increase.

In many countries, the share of tax burden paid by the financial elite has actually decreased in recent years. This is partly because of 'shadow banking', which is outside of the traditional banking systems. The worldwide shadow banking network is worth more than $80 trillion and has been growing since 2008 (in Ireland, by 2016 shadow banking had €2.3 trillion in assets, ten times the size of the Irish economy).

B

A

Common investment vehicles include private equity funds and hedge funds, which are not open to the general public but only to high-value investors. The huge extent of shadow banking is problematic because it is largely unregulated, which means more risks can be taken. In the event of another financial crisis, vast sums could be lost.

It is difficult to tax shadow banking because of its opaqueness and the fact that it is often located offshore. This means that these more speculative investments are taxed at a lower rate than safer ones.

Private equity funds focus mainly on purchasing stocks. Investors (including wealthy individuals, pension funds and foundations) form a partnership by committing money for the fund manager to invest on their behalf, usually over a ten-year term.

Hedge funds aim to achieve the highest total return for their investors and will use a wide range of techniques to do so. They are often highly leveraged and invest in a diverse range of assets that they can liquidate quickly and easily.

Effective and fair taxation is essential for a number of reasons. For example, it ensures that a degree of income redistribution takes place and it allows governments to remedy problems that markets have caused (e.g. pollution). A flat tax, whereby everyone pays the same rate regardless of income, is unlikely to be effective. Although such a tax would be simpler, it would decrease revenues and place a greater burden on lower income people.

A radical solution is a 100% inheritance tax, which would forcibly redistribute income across generations.

However, this is unworkable given the huge pressure put on governments by those opposed to such a tax, not to mention the legal and financial mechanisms that exist to decrease the tax liability of estates.

A   At the centre of this painting is Ugland House, where more than 19,000 companies are registered. It has become such a symbol of tax avoidance that Obama stated, 'Either this is the largest building in the world or the biggest tax scam on record.'

B   In 2016 Fortune 500 corporations held more than $2.6 trillion in profits offshore, where it could not be taxed.

Offshore banks are located outside of their depositors' countries of residence. They are commonly located in tax havens, jurisdictions that offer low taxation, easy access and privacy. Some of the most popular include the British Virgin Islands, the Cayman Islands, Jersey, Luxembourg and Switzerland.

A   This bank vault in Basel, Switzerland, contains 8 million 5-centime coins, one for every Swiss citizen. In 2013 the Generation Basic Income Initiative auctioned off the vault to raise money to promote the idea of basic income.

B   In 2013 the group dumped the coins in Federal Square in Bern. They wanted to gain public support for a referendum on giving everyone in Switzerland an unconditional income of 2,500 Swiss francs a month. Only 23% of voters backed the plan in 2016.

A

A possible solution is to tax financial institutions. In 2011 the British government introduced a levy on the liabilities of banks operating in Britain to discourage them from risky borrowing. Its rate peaked at 0.21% in 2015, raising around £3 billion. However, under pressure from banks, the rate is to be reduced to 0.1% between 2017 and 2022.

A more dramatic proposal is a Tobin tax, which would be levied on short-term financial transactions, particularly speculative ones. Even at a low rate (most proponents suggest 0.1–1%), it would raise billions and discourage short-term risky behaviour. Given the global nature of banking, such a tax would have to be imposed worldwide. Its critics argue that it would decrease financial transactions and investment.

The establishment of a universal basic income would alleviate poverty and redistribute wealth. Such schemes propose unconditionally offering all citizens in a country a guaranteed income. This would remove much of the apparatus of the welfare state because there would be no means testing. It would also give workers a safety net that would allow them to leave unsatisfying jobs and pursue ones that could be potentially more productive. Its critics argue it would be too expensive to implement, would lead to inflation and would have unpredictable effects on the labour market by removing the incentive to work. An alternative approach is for governments to act as an 'employer of last resort' to ensure full employment (basically a situation where every adult who is willing or able to work has a job). Under such a system the government will offer work, usually in some kind of public sector project, that provides a guaranteed and reasonable income to the persistent jobless.

Redistribution of wealth within developed countries is of paramount importance, but development economists argue that the more serious and pressing issue is the global imbalance in economic progress. Aside from its intrinsic immorality, why is it problematic that some parts of the world are becoming wealthier while others are stagnating?

B

Tobin tax James Tobin (1918–2002) was a US Keynesian economist who won the Nobel Prize in 1981. One of his most famed suggestions was a tax on foreign exchange conversions, which he argued would decrease short-term speculation. The term 'Tobin tax' now refers to all short-term transactions, regardless of what type they are.

Development economists concentrate on how to deliver growth and prosperity to poorer countries. As such, their work focuses on 'developing economies', which are the states with the lowest levels of economic output and standards of living compared to other countries. The majority of developing economies are in Africa.

A   Due to the scarcity of labour
after the US Civil War, it was
necessary to import 15,000
Chinese workers to build the
First Transcontinental Railroad
that linked the USA from coast
to coast. Here, Chinese workers
labour in 1868 at the Secret
Town trestle, built for the Central
Pacific Railroad in California.
B   Workers in the1880s build the
Northwestern Pacific Railroad.
C   Immigrants arrive at Ellis Island,
New York, in 1900.

In the future, the developing world will become increasingly important.

Emerging economies account for 80% of the world's population. As birth rates in the West steadily decline, this figure will increase. The benefits to unlocking and stimulating economic growth in these populations are huge. On one hand, if they become wealthy enough to spend money on non-essential goods and services, they represent a large potential boost to global demand. On the other hand, these populations represent a vast amount of economic potential as innovators.

The Industrial Revolution involved only one-third of the world's population. Imagine the breakthroughs in productivity that could have occurred if the entire global population had access to it.

The scale of the task of ensuring that economic progress and wealth is shared more equally on a global scale is daunting. Huge differences in wealth exist between the developed and non-developed world. Although global inequality has deep historical roots, it has not always been as dramatic as it is now. In 1500 the ratio in GDP per capita between the developed and undeveloped world was 1.3 to 1.

This increased to 6.9 to 1 by the end of the 20th century. Inequality gathered pace during the 19th and 20th centuries because some nations were able to enjoy the benefits of the Industrial Revolution and its technologies. At the same time, imperialism and colonialism led to the destruction and exploitation of many independent economies. For example, in the 18th century, India was the greatest producer of textiles in the world before it was undercut by British competition.

The means exist for developing countries to grow. The 'big push model', which originated in 1943 with the work of the economist Paul Rosenstein-Rodan (1902–85), advocates large-scale investment so that countries can gain sufficient momentum to transition from agrarian to industrialized economies and achieve long-term sustainable growth.

A major problem in the developing world is linked to its institutions. Economists Daron Acemoglu and James A. Robinson argue that this involves deep-lying historical causes relating to the nature of colonial regimes. From 1815 to 1930, more than 50 million people left Europe for other continents, particularly the Americas and Oceania (including 32.6 million to the USA, 7.2 million to Canada, 6.4 million to Argentina, 4.3 million to Brazil and 3.5 million to Australia).

Daron Acemoglu (b. 1967) is a Turkish-American economist based at the Massachusetts Institute of Technology and **James A. Robinson** (b. 1960) is a British economist based at the University of Chicago. Their book *Why Nations Fail* (2012) examines how and why states develop differently.

c

In areas where Europeans could easily settle in large numbers (e.g. Canada), democratic accountable institutions that were capable of fostering long-term economic growth were set up. In countries where climate and disease made it harder for Europeans to settle, extractive colonial regimes were put into place. They focused on exploiting the resources of these areas as much as possible. Even after decolonization and independence, the extractive nature of these regimes remains.

A   Men dig for gold in a pit in the Ituri Forest, north-eastern Democratic Republic of the Congo in 2006. The country has potentially lucrative gold deposits, but miners face corrupt government officials and security personnel who demand illegal kickbacks.

B   Children load bags of cotton onto a truck in Jizzakh, Uzbekistan, in 2010. Until 2012 the government mobilized children aged 11 to 15 to take one to two months off school to harvest the government-owned fields.

Political systems in former extractive states tend to be corrupt and unaccountable. Resources and human capital formation are not evenly distributed. This makes long-term growth nearly impossible. The problem is particularly acute in Sub-Saharan Africa, where even countries with tremendous natural resources – oil in Nigeria, bauxite in Guinea and uranium in Niger, for example – remain largely undeveloped, with only local elites and foreign companies enjoying the profits. Countries can overcome the malign legacies of imperialism, though, as seen in Botswana, which has the highest Human Development Index in Sub-Saharan Africa, and India, whose GDP rose by 7% in 2016.

A

B

The greatest adaptation that the whole world must make concerns the relationship between capitalism and the environment. Much of the progress in economic development made over the past decades will be reversed if nothing is done. According to a 2015 World Bank report, if climate change is left to continue unabated, it will drive 100 million people into poverty by 2030. Climate change could also increase the likelihood of conflict between and within nations. The Center for Climate and Security argues that this is because climate change may destabilize states by placing a strain on their ability to deliver basic services such as food, water and power, leading to internal unrest and population displacement. It may have contributed to the ongoing Syrian Civil War, which started in 2011, as drought exacerbated tensions in the country. Furthermore, in 2017 the UN Secretary General António Guterres (b. 1948) stated that addressing climate change was vital to decreasing the risk of global conflict.

A

Fossil fuels have been capitalism's main energy source since the Industrial Revolution. Reducing their use requires a fundamental political and economic shift. The Paris Agreement, drafted in 2015 and signed in 2016, commits 195 countries to work towards limiting global warming. Although this is laudable, a major problem is that there are no penalties for failure to curb emissions.

Schemes such as cap and share and tradable energy quotas provide countries with the means to reduce carbon emissions fairly over time. However, they require governments worldwide not only to commit to these schemes politically and economically by investing in the mechanisms to enforce regulations, but also to punish economic actors who break them. A further problem is that climate change has become highly politicized in many countries, particularly in the USA, where the Republican Trump administration rolled back numerous environmental regulations and pulled the USA out of the Paris Agreement.

Capitalism could provide a solution.

Just as there were incentives for British manufacturers to invest in labour-saving devices in the 18th century, thereby helping to ignite the Industrial Revolution, so too must incentives for climate change reduction be put in place. The World Bank announced in April 2016 that 28% of its future investments would be made on climate change projects such as green transportation systems, and that all future funding would account for global warming.

If renewable energy sources enjoy the same scale of research and development as non-renewable ones, the process of incremental innovation will make them more reliable, efficient and productive. This also has the potential to create millions of jobs, thereby encouraging the growth of sustainable carbon-neutral capitalism.

Tradable energy quotas (TEQs) are determined by an electronic system that assigns energy supplies a carbon rating based on the quantities of greenhouse gas they release. At the start of the year, countries are given a TEQ budget, which decreases over time. Each adult has a weekly number of free TEQ units, which are spent when carbon-producing fuel and electricity are purchased. If more units are needed, they can be purchased, and surpluses can be sold. Government and corporate users of energy have to purchase their TEQs at a weekly auction.

B

A   The Middle East's driest winter in several decades, exemplified by this dried-out gulley in the Palestinian village of al-Auja, near Jericho, in 2014, could pose a threat to global food prices, with local crops depleted along with farmers' livelihoods. In fact, varying degrees of drought are hitting almost two-thirds of the limited arable land across Syria, Lebanon, Jordan, the Palestinian territories and Iraq.
B   Environmentalists form a message of hope and peace in front of the Eiffel Tower in Paris, where the UN Climate Change Conference was being held in 2015.

ADAPTING THE CAPITALIST MODEL

The Internet can encourage innovation and economic growth. It has already revolutionized communication, allowing for the rapid dissemination of knowledge. In 1995 less than 1% of the world had access to an Internet connection. This rose to 51.7% in 2017. Developments in production and design mean that computers are becoming increasingly powerful and portable. Open-source software allows technology to be shared and improved rapidly, thereby accelerating the process of incremental innovation.

Internet use is highest in the developed world (in 2017 the country with the highest proportion of users was Japan, with 94%), but it is growing rapidly in the developing world. For example, from 2000 to 2017 the number of Internet users increased by 46,696% in Nigeria and by 66,865% in Bangladesh. Smartphones are central to this. The Internet also offers huge swathes of the world access to banking for the first time. Schemes such as M-Pesa allow people to deposit, withdraw and transfer money electronically. This addresses difficulties with cash such as theft and counterfeiting. In the future, blockchains will allow the creation of digital currencies, such as bitcoin, that are secure and transparent.

M-Pesa (the 'm' stands for mobile; pesa is Swahili for money) is a mobile banking service first launched in Kenya in 2007. It has expanded into nine other countries: Albania, Democratic Republic of the Congo, Egypt, Ghana, India, Lesotho, Mozambique, Romania and Tanzania. From 2007 to 2016, it served 29.5 million active customers and processed 6 billion transactions.

A blockchain is a secure digital ledger, first implemented in 2008. The information it records is stored on a database hosted across millions of computers, which means it is easily accessible but virtually impossible to hack because the data is decentralized. Once transactions are made, they are recorded and cannot be altered.

A   Customers do not need to have access to banks to use M-Pesa; in fact, the system is designed for such people. At M-Pesa service outlets, such as this one in Nairobi, Kenya, users deposit money that they can then access and transfer digitally using their mobile phones.

The Internet also enables the creation of international social and economic networks that were previously impossible to conceive. Theoretically, the digital economy gives certain sectors a worldwide labour market, and conversely it gives firms access to a global consumer base. Net neutrality must be maintained for this to continue.

One of the historical sources of world inequality was the uneven adoption of technology. The Internet's global and open nature must be preserved in order to avoid this being repeated with digital technology.

Bitcoin is a digital currency and was the first implementation of a blockchain. Introduced in 2009, each bitcoin is a piece of code. They are 'mined' by people who use their computers to keep track of transactions. The system is decentralized and allows direct electronic payment between users. Bitcoins are stored in a virtual wallet, secured by a password. Transactions are public but anonymous. Bitcoins can be purchased using traditional currencies through online exchanges.

Net neutrality is the principle that governments and companies should not be allowed to interfere with consumer ability to access or share information on the Internet.

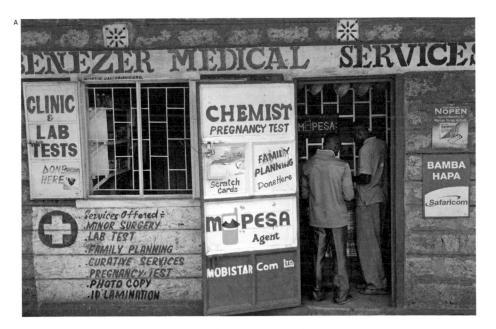

Conclusion

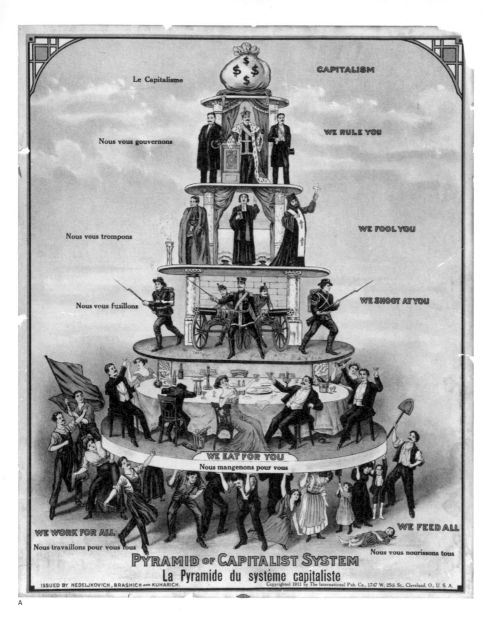

This book has set out the history, successes and failures of capitalism, as well as some of the possible alternatives to this system. The question remains: is capitalism working?

Certainly, capitalism's achievements are manifold. It has delivered more people out of poverty than any other economic system and has inspired innovations and technologies that have made our lives easier and longer. In absolute GDP per capita terms, it has steadily made the world wealthier. The average infant is now expected to live around twice as long as they were two centuries ago.

History has shown that the most sustained experiment with an alternative to capitalism, carried out in the USSR, was ultimately a failure that ended in economic stagnation and disintegration. Over the past 40 years, countries that have allowed the forces of capitalism to flourish, particularly India and China, have prospered. However, capitalism's proponents cannot simply point out the successes of the past.

B

A   The 'Pyramid of Capitalist System' was published in the *Industrial Worker* in 1911. It shows the social hierarchy supported by the labour of workers.
B   In 1938 the California Arabian Standard Oil Company (now Saudi Aramco) found a commercially viable oil well in Dhahran, on Saudi Arabia's eastern coast. The discovery transformed the Saudi Arabian economy and made the country the world's biggest exporter of oil.

A

Some of the most pressing problems the world faces are a direct result of the failures of capitalism. The system has seen human inequality of wealth rapidly increase in recent decades. This is a problem both within nations (where minority groups are still left earning less on average) and between them. Business interests have arguably played a role in destabilising some areas of the world, contributing to damaging conflicts. Capitalism has also deepened humanity's negative impact on the environment, leading to the depletion and destruction of nature as well as to climate change that may have disastrous consequences. Since its inception in the 18th and 19th centuries, the capitalist system has relied on non-renewable energy sources such as coal and petroleum. In the 21st century, it still does in many places. The future depends on the encouragement of alternative renewable sources.

There are other problems that capitalism has not solved. Although capitalism has lifted billions of people out of extreme poverty, it has not led to the elimination of the patriarchal nature of human society.

Despite the fact that gender productivity differences are non-existent in developed economies, there is a huge disparity between men and women. Female representation in senior positions is shockingly low. In 2017 only 6% of companies in the Fortune 500 list of largest US corporations had female chief executives. Furthermore, women are likely to be crowded into a smaller range of lower-paid jobs than men.

B

In general, jobs dominated by women tend to be less well-paid and prestigious than those in which men predominate. As women are more likely than men to undertake unremunerated care of dependants (particularly children), this means that they are also more likely to work part-time and therefore have a more precarious role in the workforce. A gender pay gap (the percentage difference between women's and men's average earnings) exists in every country in the world and across all economic sectors. In Britain, it is 13.9% for full-time workers. This is a global problem that is changing too slowly.

According to the World Economic Forum, at the current rate of change it will take women 170 years to receive equal pay.

A   A lone woman protests unequal pay for women in Cincinnati, Ohio, in the 1970s. During that decade, an Equal Rights Amendment fell three states short of the number necessary to add it to the US Constitution.

B   The World Economic Forum aims to bring together political and business leaders to 'improve the state of the world'. Its critics, such as those protesting in 2002 in New York, argue it is a cabal to further the interest of the elite.

A

A central feature of capitalism is inequality, but capitalism's supporters argue that inequality is not always a bad thing because it acts as an imperative, even inspirational, force. It can drive economic actors to improve, thereby encouraging innovation and increasing productivity. However, capitalism's detractors point out that inequality has unintended negative consequences, too. If it reaches too high a level, it will lead to the creation of entrenched oligarchies who may, in the long term, stifle growth by trying to preserve the system that has benefited them.

In this case, 'trickle down' economies are unlikely to enrich everyone. The elites enjoy the positive externalities of the past while not providing adequate compensation for the negative externalities of the present. In the future, both the negative and positive side effects of the capitalist system need to be more equitably shared out. This will encourage long-term growth.

Remember, an important building block in the growth of capitalism was the overthrow of governments composed of unaccountable hereditary elites. In the 21st century, they must not be allowed to be replaced by wealth-based ones. In particular, the 'Big Five' Silicon Valley firms (Amazon, Apple, Facebook, Google and Microsoft) wield increasing power and influence over our lives that, if unchecked, will grow rapidly as the digital economy becomes more significant.

Adam Smith, the first modern economist, argued that the free market would lead to the most efficient outcomes. Trusting completely in the market does not produce optimal outcomes for three main reasons.

A   Indian economic growth has delivered prosperity to millions of people, and malls like this one in Mumbai are now common. However, according to World Bank figures, in 2011 more than 20% of the population still lived below the poverty line.

B   The Chinese government has ordered the reduction of steel production as part of an effort to cut carbon emissions. However, many factories, such as this illegal steel factory in Inner Mongolia, northern China, ignore these orders and continue to operate.

B

A

Firstly, it creates a system in which the ultimate incentive is personal enrichment. This inevitably leads to short-term thinking and speculative behaviour, even when it is not the best decision for the long-term health of the economy. The crisis of 2008 showed that in an increasingly interconnected economic world, this can rapidly lead to a global disaster from which many countries are still recovering.

Secondly, as Herbert A. Simon argued, in the modern economic system organizations are more important than markets. Understanding humans as members of organizations gives a more complete view of their behaviour. People do not really identify as being a member of a market. Furthermore, they do not respond only to the incentive of profit motive; human decisions are far more complex and multi-faceted.

Thirdly, information asymmetry exists in virtually all transactions. As such, truly efficient markets cannot really exist. Even the theoretical free flow of human knowledge that the Internet provides cannot solve this problem because it cannot fully reveal personal biases and preferences.

Herbert A. Simon (1916–2001) was a US scholar who was one of the founding figures of behaviouralist economics. He made vital contributions in a number of fields, including economics, sociology, computer science, psychology and philosophy. Most of Simon's work focused on how decisions are made, for which he was awarded the Nobel Memorial Prize in Economic Sciences in 1978.

Information asymmetry occurs when one party has more (or superior) information than the other. It can be vital to securing an advantage. However, information asymmetry can cause markets to malfunction because one party knows more than the other. This can become an economic problem because it leads to buyers or sellers making sub-optimal decisions. For example, information asymmetry could lead to insurance companies raising the price of their policies because they have incomplete information about the people who have purchased them. The problem can be resolved through 'signalling' (one of the parties voluntarily conveying information) and 'screening' (the party with the disadvantage leading the other to reveal information). In 2001 the US economists George Akerlof (b. 1940), Michael Spence (b. 1943) and Joseph Stiglitz were awarded the Nobel Memorial Prize in Economic Sciences for their work in this field.

Given these imperfections, some regulation is always necessary. This is where institutions, particularly the state, come in.

Democratic governments can check the worst excesses of the market and take a long-term balanced view of the economy, while still being accountable to the people. This way, the best features of capitalism are maintained and its drawbacks are mitigated. However, a universal approach to this problem is unlikely to be effective. Generic solutions and policies will not be sufficient – local conditions and circumstances must be accounted for.

So is capitalism working? To a degree, it has already 'worked' for billions of people through the undoubted material benefits it has delivered. Yet it has also created long-term inequalities and environmental problems.

To truly assess the success or failure of capitalism, you must decide if it has provided the tools necessary to deal with the challenges of the future.

A   The 'Rich Russian Kids' Instagram account shows how the children of Russia's wealthy oligarchs live.

Further Reading

Acemoğlu, Daron and Robinson, James A., *Why Nations Fail: The Origins of Power, Prosperity and Poverty* (London: Profile, 2012)

Akerlof, George A. and Shiller, Robert J., *Animal Spirits: How Human Psychology Drives the Economy, and Why It Matters for Global Capitalism* (Princeton: Princeton University Press, 2009)

Allen, Robert C., *The British Industrial Revolution in Global Perspective* (Cambridge: Cambridge University Press, 2009)

Allen, Robert C., *Global Economic History: A Very Short Introduction* (Oxford: Oxford University Press, 2011)

Chang, Ha-Joon, *23 Things They Don't Tell You About Capitalism* (London: Allen Lane, 2010)

Chang, Ha-Joon, *Economics: The User's Guide* (London: Pelican, 2014)

Clark, Gregory, *A Farewell to Alms: A Brief Economic History of the World* (Princeton: Princeton University Press, 2007)

Datta, Saugato (ed.), *Economics: Making Sense of the Modern Economy* (3rd edition, London: The Economist in association with Profile Books, 2011)

Deaton, Angus, *The Great Escape: Health, Wealth, and the Origins of Inequality* (Princeton and Oxford: Princeton University Press, 2013)

Diamond, Jared, *Guns, Germs, and Steel: A Short History of Everybody for the Last 13,000 Years* (New York: W.W. Norton, 1997)

Gordon, Robert, *The Rise and Fall of American Growth* (Princeton: Princeton University Press, 2016)

Greenwald, Bruce C. and Kahn, Judd, *Globalization: The Irrational Fear That Someone in China Will Take Your Job* (Hoboken: John Wiley and Sons, 2009)

Harford, Tim, *The Undercover Economist* (2nd edition, London: Abacus, 2006)

Kahneman, Daniel, *Thinking, Fast and Slow* (New York: Farrar, Straus and Giroux, 2011)

Kay, John, *Other People's Money: Masters of the Universe or Servants of the People?* (London: Profile, 2015)

Klein, Naomi, *The Shock Doctrine: The Rise of Disaster Capitalism* (New York: Metropolitan Books/ Henry Holt, 2007)

Klein, Naomi, *This Changes Everything: Capitalism vs. the Climate* (London: Allen Lane, 2014)

Lanchester, John, *Whoops! Why Everyone Owes Everyone and No One Can Pay* (London: Penguin, 2010)

Lanchester, John, *How to Speak Money: What the Money People Say – And What They Really Mean* (London: Faber & Faber, 2014)

Landes, David S., *The Wealth and Poverty of Nations* (London: Abacus, 1999)

Levinson, Marc, *The Box: How the Shipping Container Made the World Smaller and the World Economy Bigger* (Princeton: Princeton University Press, 2006)

Lewis, Michael, *Flash Boys: A Wall Street Revolt* (New York: W.W. Norton, 2014)

Maddison, Angus, *Contours of the World Economy 1–2030 AD: Essays in Macro-Economic History* (Oxford: Oxford University Press, 2007)

Milanovic, Branko, *Global Inequality: A New Approach for the Age of Globalization* (Cambridge, MA: Harvard University Press, 2016)

Mokyr, Joel, *The Enlightened Economy: An Economic History of Britain 1700–1850* (New York: Yale University Press, 2009)

Mason, Paul, *Postcapitalism: A Guide to Our Future* (London: Allen Lane, 2015)

Morris, Ian, *Why the West Rules—For Now: The Patterns of History, and What They Reveal About the Future* (New York: Farrar, Straus and Giroux, 2010)

Murphy, Richard, *The Joy of Tax: How a Fair Tax System Can Create a Better Society* (London: Bantam Press, 2015)

Nayyar, Deepak, *Catch Up: Developing Countries in the World Economy* (Oxford: Oxford University Press, 2013)

North, Douglass C., *Understanding the Process of Economic Change* (Princeton: Princeton University Press, 2005)

Piketty, Thomas, *Capital in the Twenty-First Century* (Cambridge, MA: Harvard University Press, 2014)

Pomeranz, Kenneth, *The Great Divergence: China, Europe, and the Making of the Modern World Economy* (Princeton: Princeton University Press, 2000)

Rodrik, Dani, *The Globalization Paradox* (Oxford: Oxford University Press, 2011)

Sen, Amartya, *Development as Freedom* (Oxford: Oxford University Press, 1999)

Stiglitz, Joseph E., *Freefall: Free Markets and the Sinking of the Global Economy* (London: Penguin, 2010)

Stiglitz, Joseph E., *The Price of Inequality: How Today's Divided Society Endangers Our Future* (New York: W.W. Norton, 2012)

Stiglitz, Joseph E. and Greenwald, Bruce C., *Creating a Learning Society: A New Approach to Growth, Development, and Social Progress* (New York: Columbia University Press, 2014)

Valdez, Stephen and Molyneux, Philip, *An Introduction to Global Financial Markets* (7th edition, Basingstoke: Palgrave Macmillan, 2013)

Vigna, Paul and Casey, Michael J., *Cryptocurrency: How Bitcoin and Digital Money Are Challenging the Global Economic Order* (London: Bodley Head, 2015)

Wolman, David, *The End of Money: Counterfeiters, Preachers, Techies, Dreamers – and the Coming Cashless Society* (Boston: Da Capo, 2012)

Wrigley, E. A., *Energy and the English Industrial Revolution* (Cambridge: Cambridge University Press, 2010)

Picture Credits

a = above, b = below,
c = centre, l = left, r = right

2 Courtesy Dan Tague
4–5 Paulo Whitaker / Reuters
6–7 Visions of America, LLC / Alamy Stock Photo
8 Courtesy Halas & Batchelor
11 De Agostini / G. Cigolini / Veneranda Biblioteca Ambrosiana / Bridgeman Images
12 Maersk Line
13 Simon Dawson / Bloomberg via Getty Images
14 a Doha, Qatar, 1980s
14 b Doha, Qatar, 2000s
15 l Issouf Sanogo / AFP / Getty Images
15 r Robert Matton AB / Alamy Stock Photo
16–17 Alte Nationalgalerie, Berlin
18 Private collection
19 Private collection
20 l Private collection
20 r Yale Center for British Art, Paul Mellon Collection
21 l SSPL / Getty Images

21 r Fox Photos / Getty Images
22 Library of Congress, Washington, D.C.
23 Florilegius / Alamy Stock Photo
24 a Michel Porro / Getty Images
24 c Hulton Archive / Getty Images
24 b The Trustees of the British Museum, London
25 Private collection
26 DEA Picture Library / De Agostini / Getty Images
27 The Granger Collection / Alamy Stock Photo
28 British Library, London
29 l Private collection
29 r Private collection
30 National Portrait Gallery, London
31 Courtesy Classical Numismatic Group, Inc., www.cngcoins.com
32 Anindito Mukherjee / Reuters
33 Henrique Alvim Corrêa
34 Courtesy Lamptech
35 Rykoff Collection / Getty Images
36 World History Archive / Alamy Stock Photo
37 l Private collection
37 r Universal Images Group / Universal History Archive / Diomedia
38 Popperfoto / Getty Images
39 Margaret Bourke-White / Getty Images
40 l Hulton-Deutsch Collection / Corbis via Getty Images

41 Bettmann / Getty Images
42 Smith Collection / Gado / Getty Images
43 Everett Collection Historical / Alamy Stock Photo
44 The Conservative Party Archive / Getty Images
45 Süddeutsche Zeitung Photo / Alamy Stock Photo
46 © European Communities, 1993 / E.C. - Audiovisual Service / Photo Christian Lambiotte
47 Sion Touhig / Sygma via Getty Images
48 Chris Ratcliffe / Getty Images
49 Warrick Page / Getty Images
50–51 Stuart Franklin / Magnum Photos
52 Musée d'Orsay, Paris
53 British Library, London
54 New Holland Agriculture
55 Agencja Fotograficzna Caro / Alamy Stock Photo
56 l United States Patent Office
56 r United States Patent Office
57 Courtesy Allphones
58 a Zuma / Diomedia
58 b Zuma / Rex / Shutterstock
59 a, b Doug Coombe
60 Bettmann / Getty Images
61 Darryn Lyons / Associated Newspapers / Rex / Shutterstock
62 Fine Art Images / Diomedia
63 Pictures from History / akg Images
64 a, b Michael Seleznev / Alamy Stock Photo

65 Ferdinando Scianna /
　Magnum Photos
66 Greg Baker / AP / Rex /
　Shutterstock
67 l, r From *Measuring Economic
　Growth from Outer Space*,
　J. Vernon Henderson, Adam
　Storeygard, David N. Weil.
　NBER Working Paper No.
　15199, 2011
68 a Harald Hauswald /
　Ostkreuz
68 b Herbert Maschke, *Street
　scene at Café Kranzler*, 1962.
　Stiftung Stadtmuseum Berlin,
　Morlind Tumler / Cornelius
　Maschke. Reproduction
　Cornelius Maschke
69 Imaginechina / Rex /
　Shutterstock
70 Sandry Anggada
71 Sebastián Vivallo Oñate
　/ Agencia Makro /
　LatinContent / Getty Images
72 Yvan Cohen / LightRocket via
　Getty Images
73 Kham / Reuters
74–75 Kevin Frayer / Getty
　Images
76 Mail Online
77 Fox Photos / Getty Images
78 Sinopix / Rex / Shutterstock
79 Kristoffer Tripplaar / Alamy
　Stock Photo
80 Frans Hals Museum, Haarlem,
　Netherlands
81 Thomas Locke Hobbs
82 a, c, b AFP / Getty Images
83 Rex / AP / Shutterstock

84 Artem Samokhvalov /
　Shutterstock
85 Kazuhiro Nogi / AFP / Getty
　Images
86 l Private collection
86 r Courtesy Nathan Mandreza
87 l Courtesy Lalo Alcaraz
87 r Jeanne Verdoux,
　jeanneverdoux.com
88 Daniel Leal-Olivas / AFP /
　Getty Images
89 Chris Barker, christhebarker.
　tumblr.com
90 l Marianne
90 r Der Spiegel
91 Milos Bicanski / Getty Images
92 M/Y *Eclipse*, builder
　Blohm+Voss, designer
　Terence Disdale
93 l Jean-Pierre Muller / AFP /
　Getty Images
93 r Simon Dawson / Bloomberg
　via Getty Images
94–95 Lukas Schulze / Getty
　Images
96 a, b Courtesy Cordaid
97 Rex / AP / Shutterstock
98 Romeo Gacad / AFP / Getty
　Images
99 Li Feng / Getty Images
100–101 Aly Song / Reuters
102 Robert Schediwy
103 l, r Landsberger Collection,
　International Institute of
　Social History, Amsterdam
104 Reuters
105 Carlos Barria / Reuters
106 © Walker Evans Archive, The
　Metropolitan Museum of Art,

　New York
107 Oli Scarff / Getty Images
108 Courtesy Harrods Bank
109 Scott Olson / Getty Images
110 l mikeledray / Shutterstock
110 r Jeremy Brooks
111 a Doran
111 b mikeledray / Shutterstock
112 Nicholas Kamm / AFP / Getty
　Images
113 meinzahn / 123rf.com
114 © Paolo Woods and Gabriele
　Galimberti
115 Bruce Rolff / Shutterstock
116 Ruben Sprich / Reuters
117 Denis Balibouse / Reuters
118 l Granger Historical Picture
　Archive / Alamy Stock Photo
118 r Bettmann / Getty Images
119 Library of Congress,
　Washington, D.C.
120 Randy Olson / National
　Geographic / Getty Images
121 Carolyn Drake / Magnum
　Photos
122 Ammar Awad / Reuters
123 Benoit Tessier / Reuters
125 Benedicte Desrus / Alamy
　Stock Photo
126–127 Steve McCurry /
　Magnum Photos
128 Private collection
129 914 collection / Alamy Stock
　Photo
130 Cincinnati Museum Center /
　Getty Images
131 Alex Majoli / Magnum Photos
132 Radu Bercan / Shutterstock
133 Kevin Frayer / Getty Images

Index

References to illustrations
are in **bold**.

Acknowledgments:
The author would like to thank the team of editors
and designers at Thames & Hudson who made this
book happen, and colleagues at the University of
Cambridge for all the invigorating discussion and
debate about the process of economic change.

This book is dedicated to my goddaughter Bel
and godson Billy.

Is Capitalism Working? © 2018
Thames & Hudson Ltd, London

General Editor: Matthew Taylor
Text by Jacob Field

For image copyright information, see pp. 138–139

First published in 2018 in the United States of
America by Thames & Hudson Inc., 500 Fifth
Avenue, New York, New York 10110

Library of Congress Control Number: 2018932293

ISBN 978-0-500-29367-6

Printed and bound in Hong Kong through Asia
Pacific Offset Ltd